Young Person's Occupational Outlook Handbook

Descriptions for America's Top 250 Jobs

Based on the U.S. Department of Labor's
Occupational Outlook Handbook

JIST Works, Inc.

Young Person's Occupational Outlook Handbook

©1996 by JIST Works, Inc.

Published by JIST Works, Inc.
720 N. Park Avenue
Indianapolis, IN 46202-3431
Phone: 317-264-3720 Fax: 317-264-3709 E-mail: JISTWorks@AOL.com

Cover Illustration by Richard Scott Morris

Printed in the United States of America

99 98 97   9 8 7 6 5 4 3

Library of Congress Cataloging-in-Publication Data
Young person's occupational outlook handbook.
       p.   cm.
  Descriptions of occupations are based on those found in the
Occupational outlook handbook.
    ISBN 1-56370-201-0: $19.95
     1. Occupations. 2. Job descriptions. 3. Vocational guidance.
  I. Occupational outlook handbook.
  HF5382.Y58   1996   95-26613
  331.7'02—dc20   CIP

We have been careful to provide accurate information throughout this book, but it is possible that errors and omissions have been introduced. Please consider this in making any career plans or other important decisions. Trust your own judgment above all else and in all things.

ISBN 1-56370-201-0

Introduction

This book was developed to help you explore a wide variety of jobs. This is important because career decisions are some of the most important decisions you will make.

The Young Person's Occupational Outlook Handbook answers questions such as: How is this job done? What training will I need to do this job? Where will I work? How much money will I earn? Will this job be in demand in the future?

The descriptions in the book are based on those found in a book titled the *Occupational Outlook Handbook (OOH)*. The *OOH* is revised every two years by the U.S. Department of Labor and is the most widely used source of career information available. Like the *OOH*, this book groups similar jobs together. This approach makes it easy to explore related jobs you might not otherwise consider. Since the descriptions in the *OOH* are longer than the ones in this book, you can refer to the *OOH* for additional information on jobs that most interest you.

Tips on Identifying Jobs That Interest You

In the Table of Contents at the beginning of this book, jobs are arranged into 14 clusters. Select one or more of the clusters that interest you most by looking at the types of jobs listed in each cluster. As you do, note (on a separate piece of paper) any jobs within those clusters that look particularly interesting. Then read about the jobs that interest you.

Information Provided in Each Job Description

Each one-page entry in this book includes the following:

Job Description: This is a short explanation of the duties and activities involved in the job. It describes the worker's responsibilities and major areas of specialization.

Something Extra: An interesting fact or detail is highlighted for each job, including historical, technical, and scientific information.

Working Conditions: Details about the job, such as the number of hours worked each week, if evening or weekend work is required, physical requirements, and possible health hazards.

Subjects to Study: Lists courses that will help prepare you for the job.

Discover More: Includes activities that can help you find out if you will enjoy similar jobs. For example, you might be encouraged to interview someone who holds the type of job that interests you, to visit a worksite where that work is done, or to do volunteer work that requires similar skills.

Related Jobs: Lists jobs that use similar skills, talents, or interests. Some of these jobs may require more or less education or training than the job you are reading about.

Earnings: Each job is rated according to how much money an experienced worker can expect to make in one year. Beginning workers will often earn much less, and pay rates are lower in some parts of the country, so use these figures only as a guideline.*

Very Low	Less than $20,000 a year
Low	$21,000 to $25,000 a year
Average	$26,000 to $35,000 a year
High	$36,000 to $45,000 a year
Very High	$45,000 or more a year

Education and Training: This section describes what kind of degree or training you need to get the job. Note that most jobs have people working in them with less or more education or training than indicated here.*

High School—No specialized training is needed for this job

Specialized Training—Requires on-the-job training, apprenticeship, or short training lasting from several months to less than two years

Associate degree—Requires two years of coursework in a college or technical school

Bachelor's degree—Requires four years of coursework in a college or university

Master's degree—Requires one or two years additional coursework beyond a bachelor's degree

Doctorate degree—Requires two or more years of education beyond a master's degree

Professional degree—These degrees are related to a particular profession, such as those required to be an attorney or physician. They require two to six years of education beyond a bachelor's degree

Job Outlook: Tells you how much the job is expected to grow and employ people in the years to come. Usually, the faster a job is projected to grow, the better the opportunities for employment in that job. Here are the terms used in each description and what they mean:*

Increasing Rapidly—Employment opportunities are projected to grow rapidly in the future

Increasing—Employment opportunities in this job are expected to grow at an average or somewhat above average rate in the future

Little Change—Employment opportunities in this job are expected to remain about the same in the future

Decreasing—Employment opportunities in this career are expected to grow very slowly or decline in the future

Some Things to Consider in Making a Career Decision

Planning your career is one of the most important things you will do in your life. Your decisions will affect your everyday life for many years to come. By exploring career options now, you will be better prepared to make good decisions later. Here are some things to consider in exploring career alternatives:

Interests: If a job seems interesting to you, that is enough reason to find out more about it. For example, if you are interested in music, you might find that a job in the music industry would be just right for you.

Values: It is important to look for a job that allows you to do things that you believe in. For example, if you want to help people, you will be happier in a job that allows you to do that.

Pay: How much you earn in a job will be important since it affects what kind of lifestyle you can afford. Higher paying jobs often require higher levels of education or training, or higher levels of responsibility.

Working Conditions: Do you like to work indoors or outdoors? Would you rather work by yourself, in a group, or be in charge? What kinds of people do you like to spend time with? These and other things should be considered in your job choice.

Satisfaction: You will spend many hours working, and you will be more satisfied with work that you enjoy. Think about the things you enjoy and are good at, such as classes you take, hobbies, family activities, volunteer work, past jobs you've had, and other life experiences. What did you like about these activities? These will provide you with clues for job possibilities.

Skills: What skills do you have? What are you good at? For example, if you are good at organizing social events, can you think of any jobs that might require this skill?

Education and Training: How much training or education are you willing to consider? Most of the better-paying jobs these days require education or training beyond high school. And more and more jobs now require computer or technical skills. Consider any job that interests you, even if you don't know how you will afford the training or education needed for it.

Self-Employment: More than 10 percent of people in the workforce are either self-employed or running their own businesses. There are many books on this topic. If this option interests you, learn more about it!

Getting More Information

Once you have found one or more jobs in the book that interest you, you can find out more about them in a number of ways. The *Occupational Outlook Handbook* includes more detailed descriptions for each of the jobs described here. A book titled *America's Top 300 Jobs* provides the same descriptions found in the *OOH.* Both of these books can be found in most libraries or bookstores. A librarian can show you many other career resource materials. Also consider interviewing people who work in the jobs that interest you. They will tell you how to get started in the field, what education or training is needed, what they do and do not like about the job, and many other details.

*A handy key to the categories in this book is included on the inside back cover.

Contents

Professional Specialty Occupations

Technicians and Related Support Occupations

Marketing and Sales Occupations

Administrative Support Occupations, Including Clerical

Service Occupations

Agriculture, Forestry, Fishing and Related Occupations

Mechanics, Installers, and Repairers

Construction Trades and Extractive Occupations

Production Occupations

Transportation and Material Moving Occupations

Job Opportunities in the Armed Forces

Executive, Administrative, and Managerial Occupations

Accountants and Auditors

Job Description

Accountants and auditors prepare financial reports and taxes. They also check the financial reports and taxes of others. They work for businesses and other organizations, the government, and individuals. Computers are widely used in accounting and auditing.

Working Conditions

Accountants and auditors spend much of their time in offices. Sometimes they travel to clients' offices to conduct audits. Some self-employed accountants work from their homes. A 40-hour week is normal. During tax season, tax specialists work long hours.

Subjects to Study

English, mathematics, speech, business, computer skills

Discover More

Test your accounting skills. Ask your parents to let you try balancing their checking account. A checking account is a simple bookkeeping record. The instructions for balancing the account are usually printed on the back of the bank statement.

Related Jobs

Appraisers, budget officers, loan officers, financial analysts and managers, bank officers, actuaries, underwriters, tax collectors and revenue agents, FBI special agents, securities sales workers, and purchasing agents

Earnings	Education and Training	Job Outlook

Average	Bachelor's	Increasing

Administrative Services Managers

Job Description

Administrative services managers work for private businesses and government agencies. They are in charge of supportive services such as secretarial, payroll, travel and conference planning, mail, buying and selling property, food, security, and parking. In a large business, they may supervise others. In a small business, they may be responsible for all supportive services.

Working Conditions

Administrative services managers work in offices that may be crowded and noisy. A 40-hour week is normal; however, problems may mean overtime is necessary. Travel may be a part of this job. These managers may get stressed when trying to meet deadlines.

Subjects to Study

English, mathematics, speech, computer skills, business

Discover More

Practice your organizational skills by planning a time schedule of your week. Divide the week into days. Set some goals for the week. Under each day, list your activities for that day. During the week, check off the activities you get done. By week's end, what goals have you reached?

Related Jobs

Administrative assistants, appraisers, buyers, clerical supervisors, contract specialists, cost estimators, procurement services managers, property and real estate managers, purchasing managers, marketing and sales managers, and personnel managers

Earnings	Education and Training	Job Outlook
Average	Associate/Bachelor's	Decreasing

Budget Analysts

Job Description

Budget analysts put together financial plans. They estimate the amount of money an organization needs to work effectively and make a profit. They set up annual budgets for an entire year. Throughout the year, they check reports and accounts to make sure the budget is being used correctly. Budget analysts are employed by private industries and by government agencies.

Working Conditions

Budget analysts work independently in offices. A 40-hour work week is normal. Deadlines may mean over-time and stress. Some travel may be required.

Subjects to Study

Mathematics, English, business, economics, computer skills, sociology

Discover More

Learn how you get and use money. Make a column listing categories such as allowance, monetary gifts, lawn mowing, and babysitting. These are ways you get money. In the next column list categories such as entertainment, personal and school supplies, food, and savings. These are ways you use money. For one month, keep a record of the amount of money you get and use.

Related Jobs

Accountants and auditors, economists, financial analysts, financial managers, and loan officers

Earnings	Education and Training	Job Outlook

High	Bachelor's	Little change

Construction and Building Inspectors

Job Description

Construction and building inspectors check the quality and safety of roads, water systems, and all types of structures. Some inspectors specialize in areas such as electrical work, plumbing, elevators, and mechanical appliances. Home inspectors may be hired by home buyers to report on the condition of a house before it is purchased. Inspectors are responsible for enforcing local and state laws called building codes.

Something Extra

Before the carnival opens, all amusement rides must be inspected and meet certain safety standards. Skiers using ski lifts are protected by required safety inspections. The same inspectors who check elevators and escalators may evaluate the safety of these recreational devices.

Working Conditions

Construction and building inspectors work alone from field offices writing reports and letters. Other work time is spent at the construction site. Wearing a hard hat for safety, the inspector may need to climb high ladders or crawl into tight places. If a construction accident occurs, an inspector may be called immediately.

Subjects to Study

Mathematics, geometry, algebra, English, drafting, shop courses, computer skills

Discover More

Photographs are often used in inspection reports. Practice taking some photos of buildings around your neighborhood. Try focusing on some of the building details.

Related Jobs

Drafters, estimators, industrial engineering technicians, and surveyors

Earnings	Education and Training	Job Outlook
Average	High school/Associate	Increasing

Construction Contractors and Managers

Something Extra

Building materials vary from country to country depending on the products available. In China, for instance, lots of stone and brick are used for construction because much of the land is treeless. Tile roofs there are both decorative and fire-proof. Pagodas, which resemble small towers, have been constructed of brick, stone, iron, and even porcelain.

Job Description

Construction contractors and managers plan, budget, and direct construction projects. They ensure that all legal permits and licenses are obtained. They hire workers and set timetables to complete each step of the project. They make sure that building materials are delivered to construction sites on time. They are responsible for the overall safety of the job site.

Working Conditions

Construction contractors and managers are "on call" to deal with problems. A normal 40-hour week is rare. They work from a main office or a field office at the construction site. Traveling may be involved. Overseas projects may mean living in another country for a period of time.

Subjects to Study

Mathematics, English, business, computer science, drafting, technology programs

Discover More

Do you enjoy working with wood, landscaping, electricity, or plumbing? Develop a technical skill that you enjoy. You may do this by joining particular clubs, taking special school classes, or asking an adult who is skilled in your interest area to help you.

Related Jobs

Architects, civil engineers, construction supervisors, cost engineers, cost estimators, developers, electrical engineers, industrial engineers, landscape architects, mechanical engineers

Earnings	Education and Training	Job Outlook

Average	Bachelor's	Increasing rapidly

Cost Estimators

Job Description

Cost estimators work for both construction and manufacturing companies. They gather information about the cost of materials, workers, machinery, and other business expenses. Business owners use this data to figure out their cost in producing or building a project. Cost estimators use computers because their work involves many complex mathematical techniques.

Working Conditions

Cost estimators work in offices, at construction work sites, and on the factory floor. A 40-hour week is normal, but overtime is often required. The pressure to be accurate and ensure a profit is always present.

Something Extra

When a company is deciding whether to make a new product, a cost estimator determines the least expensive way to make the best product. First, the estimator must know all the materials and machinery needed to make the product. Possible suppliers will be contacted for price information. Labor hours to produce the product will be estimated. After much study, a product may or may not be added to the line.

Subjects to Study

Mathematics, English, computer science, technology programs

Discover More

Think of a craft or food product that you could make and sell. What will all the materials and labor cost to make your product? (Include every aspect of making the product.) How much profit do you want to make? How much will you charge? Will people pay that price?

Related Jobs

Appraisers, cost accountants, cost engineers, economists, evaluators, financial analysts, loan officers, operation research analysts, underwriters, and value engineers

Earnings	Education and Training	Job Outlook
Low	Associate/Bachelor's	Increasing

Education Administrators

Something Extra

Education administration is not an entry-level job. A person employed in an entry-level job has only the minimum training or educational requirements. Sometimes no experience is necessary. Usually, an educational administrator seeks additional education and works in a related occupation for many years to gain experience.

Job Description

Education administrators give leadership and direction to schools, colleges and universities, and other community educational organizations on a daily basis. They communicate with teachers and other school staff, parents, students, and community leaders. They develop educational goals and see that they are met. They prepare budgets. Education administrators may be school principals, college deans, or school superintendents.

Working Conditions

Fast-paced, stimulating, stressful, and demanding are words describing this job. Education administrators work more than 40 hours each week. They attend school activities on weeknights and weekends, work year-round, and may travel.

Subjects to Study

Mathematics, English, speech, computer science, statistics, psychology, college preparatory subjects such as science, history

Discover More

Attend a local school board meeting. It should be open to the public. Think about the topics that the school board deals with during the meeting. These are items that the school superintendent and other school administrators will have to enforce.

Related Jobs

Health service administrators, social service agency administrators, recreation and park managers, museum directors, library directors, professional and membership organization executives

Earnings	Education and Training	Job Outlook

High	Master's/Doctorate	Little change

Employment Interviewers

Job Description

Employment interviewers help job seekers find jobs and employers find workers. They try to find the right worker for each job and the right job for each worker. They must be able to convince employers to let their agency supply workers. They may help hard-to-place job seekers get training or additional skills to do the jobs they want to do.

Working Conditions

Employment interviewers usually work in offices. Working at a computer terminal is common. They may travel to the employers' offices to place their applicants in jobs. Some may work overtime when jobs must be filled immediately.

Something Extra

Some employment interviewers are called head hunters. These interviewers contact highly skilled individuals such as lawyers, accountants, and computer specialists to add to their list of available workers. Because they actively hunt for additional people or "heads" to offer to employers, they came to be called head hunters.

Subjects to Study

Mathematics, English, speech, computer skills, business

Discover More

A skill is something you can do well. You may have hundreds of skills you don't even know about yet! Make a list of the skills you know you have. These can be physical, academic, and social skills. If you were a job interviewer, what job would you suggest for a person with your skills?

Related Jobs

Personnel officers, career counselors, community and vocational counselors

Earnings	Education and Training	Job Outlook
Low	Bachelor's	Increasing

Engineering, Science, and Data Processing Managers

Job Description

Engineering, science, and data processing managers plan and direct research, new product development, and computer programs. They supervise highly skilled individuals such as engineers, scientists, and computer specialists. They make detailed plans involving the cost, equipment, and people needed for projects.

Working Conditions

Engineering, science, and data processing managers work in offices, laboratories, and industrial plants. A 40-hour week is normal, with additional hours when deadlines must be met. Pressure to meet goals within a short time or with a limited budget may occur.

Subjects to Study

Mathematics, English, physical sciences, physics, chemistry, technology courses, computer skills

Discover More

Learn how to organize a project. Create a peanut butter factory. Make a list of the materials and equipment you will need. What kind and how many workers will you need? Draw "blueprints" or a design of the way you would produce a jar of peanut butter.

Related Jobs

Engineers, natural scientists, computer personnel, mathematicians, general managers, top executives

Earnings	Education and Training	Job Outlook

High	Master's	Increasing

Financial Managers

Job Description

Financial managers write reports that businesses use to operate. They make sure that the business pays the right amount of taxes and has enough money to operate. They provide information about the company's current spending as well as future spending. Financial managers communicate with investors about the firm's finances.

Working Conditions

Financial managers work in comfortable offices. A 40-hour work week is normal. Overtime is sometimes required. Attending meetings of local and national financial associations may be expected.

Something Extra

Many businesses have customers in foreign countries. Business procedures in foreign countries are different than in the United States. To learn about these differences, financial managers must continue their education. Continuing education is training after a person has already earned a degree. Businesses often give employees such training, or pay for university classes that will benefit employees on the job.

Subjects to Study

Mathematics, English, writing skills, speech, computer skills, psychology, business, accounting

Discover More

Do you have a checking or savings account? If so, each time you receive a statement, check it to make sure it agrees with the amount of money you have in the account. Many times a financial manager will oversee the accuracy of the bank statements you receive.

Related Jobs

Accountants and auditors, budget officers, credit analysts, loan officers, insurance consultants, portfolio managers, pension consultants, real estate advisors, securities analysts, underwriters

Earnings	Education and Training	Job Outlook
High	Bachelor's	Little change

Funeral Directors

Something Extra

Embalmment is the practice of treating bodies to prevent decay. Embalmers prepare the body by washing it with special soap and replace blood with embalming fluid, which acts as a preservative. Cosmetics or reconstructive materials such as clay, cotton, or wax may be used to make the body appear more natural. Embalmers dress the body and place it in a casket.

Job Description

Funeral directors (also called morticians or undertakers) prepare bodies for burial or cremation. Most funeral directors are also trained, licensed, and practicing embalmers. They handle the paperwork after someone dies, comfort family and friends, and help plan the funeral and burial arrangements. Funeral directors also make sure that their business is making a profit.

Working Conditions

Funeral directors work long, irregular hours including evenings and weekends. They must follow strict health regulations to protect themselves from infectious diseases. Funeral directors must be well groomed and dress conservatively in suits and ties or dresses.

Subjects to Study

Mathematics, English, speech, writing skills, psychology, business, biology, chemistry

Discover More

To learn more about a funeral director's work, talk to a local funeral director. Find out what type of training is available in your area. You may be able to get a part-time or summer job at a funeral home, doing maintenance work and cleaning limousines and hearses.

Related Jobs

Clergymen and women, social workers, psychologists, psychiatrists, health care professionals

Earnings	Education and Training	Job Outlook

Average	Specialized training/Professional degree	Little change

General Managers and Top Executives

Job Description

General managers and top executives keep a business operating efficiently while it is making a profit. Top executives help decide a company's goals and how to reach them. They may meet with executives of other corporations, domestic or foreign governments, or outside consultants to discuss things that could affect their corporation's policies. General managers are responsible for their own departments within a large organization.

Something Extra

Companies sometimes "downsize" to become more profitable. Downsizing means that the company tries to continue to do the same work with fewer people. The company may have to "restructure." Restructuring means the company changes the way it operates. Many general managers and top executives have lost their jobs due to downsizing and restructuring in recent years.

Working Conditions

General managers and top executives work in offices. Although their schedules may be flexible, they usually work long hours including weekends and nights. Travel is often necessary. Job transfers to other cities and foreign countries are common. Because executives in charge of unprofitable companies may lose their jobs, they're pressured to be productive and profitable.

Subjects to Study

Mathematics, English, speech, business, accounting, computer science, psychology

Discover More

Take a leadership position in an organization of which you are a member. Examples are speech club, drama club, music ensembles, and athletic teams. Other organizations include 4-H, FFA, and scouting. Review the organization's goals or help set some goals. Then find ways to achieve those goals.

Related Jobs

Governor, mayor, postmaster, commissioner, director, office chief

Earnings	Education and Training	Job Outlook

Very high	Bachelor's/Master's/Professional degree	Decreasing

Government Chief Executives and Legislators

Job Description

Government chief executives and legislators serve at the local, state, and national levels of government. They're either elected by the people or appointed by other government officials. Chief executives are responsible for how the government operates. They appoint department heads such as police chiefs and finance directors. Legislators are elected to make laws that solve problems and promote beneficial activities.

Working Conditions

Government chief executives are on call at all times to handle emergencies. They work full-time the entire year. The hours vary greatly depending on the size of the area being served. State legislators work full-time during the legislative sessions and part-time the rest of the year. Local officials may work part-time. Much travel may be needed to keep in touch with other government officials and the people being served.

Subjects to Study

Mathematics, English, speech, writing skills, psychology, government, history

Discover More

Run for a class or club office. Set some goals that you would strive for if you were elected to office. This will be your "platform." Organize your campaign with those goals in mind. You may need to choose a running mate to help you carry out your goals.

Related Jobs

Corporate chief executives and board members, military generals

Earnings	Education and Training	Job Outlook

High	Bachelor's	Little change

Health Services Managers

Job Description

Health services managers plan and supervise others' health care. Top administrators and assistants meet government regulations, plan new services, and involve the community. At the same time they ensure the facility is financially stable. In a small facility such as a nursing home, managers make day-to-day decisions. Other health service managers are responsible for one area, such as the physical therapy department.

Working Conditions

Health care managers may work long hours. Because hospitals and nursing homes are open 24 hours a day, they must be on call at all times. They may need to travel to attend meetings or to check on other facilities that are part of the health organization.

Something Extra

Many people use a Health Maintenance Organization (HMO) to pay for health care. Individuals or their employers pay a set amount of money to the HMO which entitles them to medical care. Certain doctors, dentists, and other health care providers belong to the HMO. Participants may get medical services from these health care providers for a lesser cost. Health services managers sometimes organize these HMO programs.

Subjects to Study

Mathematics, English, speech, writing skills, business, psychology, health careers, health

Discover More

Medical services is one of the fastest growing industries in the country. If you are interested in this field, check with a local nursing home or hospital about their volunteer program. You may learn more about the health field and patient care while helping others.

Related Jobs

Public health directors, social welfare administrators, directors of voluntary health agencies and health professional associations, underwriters in health insurance companies and HMOs

Earnings	Education and Training	Job Outlook
High	Bachelor's/Master's	Increasing

Hotel Managers and Assistants

Job Description

Hotel managers and assistants make sure that hotel guests enjoy their stay. Hotel managers are responsible for efficient and profitable operations. General managers are responsible for the overall operation of the hotel. They set room rates, approve budgets, and establish standards of quality for hotel services. Other managers oversee hotel operations such as housekeeping, room reservations, conventions, and food service.

Something Extra

Each year vacationers board floating hotels called cruise ships. Cruise ships travel through exotic areas of the world while passengers enjoy all the luxuries of a hotel stay. Dining, dancing, live entertainment, volleyball, jogging, and swimming are just part of the trip. Guests can also shop for souvenirs of their cruise in shops on the ship.

Working Conditions

Hotel managers usually work more than 40 hours each week. Because hotels are open 24 hours a day every day of the year, night and weekend work is normal. Resort hotels may only be open during the tourist season. These managers may have different jobs during the "off" season. Dealing with unhappy guests and large groups causes pressure and stress.

Subjects to Study

Mathematics, English, speech, business, accounting, economics, psychology, home economics, technology skills, computer skills

Discover More

Plan a meal for your family. Make a grocery list of the ingredients you will need. Prepare the meal and set a serving time. Serve the meal and clean up the serving area and kitchen. Can you imagine all the work involved in preparing a banquet for 250 people?

Related Jobs

Restaurant managers, apartment building managers, retail store and office managers

Earnings	Education and Training	Job Outlook

Low	Specialized training/Bachelor's	Little change

Industrial Production Managers

Job Description

Industrial production managers find the best ways to produce their factory's goods. They make sure there are enough workers and materials, proper equipment is used, and enough product is produced. They decide on the sequence in which a product will be made. They check the product quality to make sure it meets company standards and maintain inventory levels to meet customer demands.

Working Conditions

Industrial production managers work in offices and in factories. They usually work more than 40 hours a week. In factories that operate around the clock, they may work in shifts or be "on call" to deal with emergencies. They may have to stay at work until the problem is solved.

Something Extra

Industrial production managers must know the particular factory in which they work. They may spend several months in a company training program before actually starting their duties. The program helps them learn about the production line, the company's policies, and the job requirements. They may also work in other departments such as accounting or purchasing to learn about the company.

Subjects to Study

Mathematics, English, writing skills, computer skills, speech

Discover More

Plan a craft project. List all the materials you need to make the project and where to get them. Doing an inventory like this is an important part of this job.

Related Jobs

Sales engineers, manufacturers' sales representatives, industrial engineers

Earnings	Education and Training	Job Outlook
Very high	Bachelor's/Professional degree	Little change

Inspectors and Compliance Officers, except Construction

Job Description

Inspectors and compliance officers enforce laws for public protection. Their duties vary greatly. Some inspectors work with health and safety laws, while others deal with immigration laws. Some make sure that food, water, and air are cleaner. These inspectors can be found in fields such as agriculture, aviation, customs, immigration, logging, mining, and transportation.

Working Conditions

Inspectors work inside and outside in many different environments. They often travel in a car owned by the company. Their jobs can be dangerous and unpleasant; they may be exposed to hazards or deal with criminal activities. They work long and often irregular hours.

Subjects to Study

Mathematics, English, speech, writing skills, science, health

Discover More

Do your part to protect the environment. Start your family on recycling. Be a part of Earth Day—a special day planned to make people aware of ways to protect and preserve our natural resources.

Related Jobs

Construction and building inspectors, fire marshals, state and local police officers, FBI and Secret Service agents, fish and game wardens

Earnings	Education and Training	Job Outlook

Average	Specialized training/Bachelor's	Increasing

Loan Officers and Counselors

Job Description

Loan officers help people gather financial information and fill out loan applications. This information helps them decide whether or not to give loans. Loan counselors help people with low incomes or poor credit get loans. They help people set up a budget to pay back their debts. Loan officers and counselors must keep abreast of new financial products and services that will meet their customers' needs.

Working Conditions

Loan officers and counselors work in offices. Some loan officers may travel. A 40-hour week is normal, but they may work longer. They are busiest when interest rates are low and more people are applying for loans.

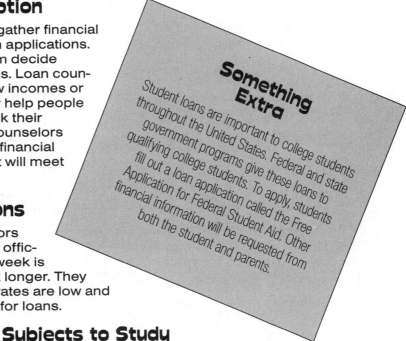

Something Extra

Student loans are important to college students throughout the United States. Federal and state government programs give these loans to qualifying college students. To apply, students fill out a loan application called the Free Application for Federal Student Aid. Other financial information will be requested from both the student and parents.

Subjects to Study

Mathematics, English, speech, writing skills, business, computer skills, accounting, psychology

Discover More

Ask your parents to show you a credit card application or get one at your local bank. (These applications also often come in the mail.) Filling out a credit card application is like filling out a loan application because the information requested is often the same.

Related Jobs

Securities and financial services sales representatives, financial aid officers, real estate agents and brokers, insurance agents and brokers

Earnings	Education and Training	Job Outlook
Average	Bachelor's	Increasing

Management Analysts and Consultants

Something Extra

When a company needs a specialist or wants advice from someone outside the business, it may hire a consultant. Consultants are not usually company employees. Many consultants are self-employed and may have more flexible work schedules because they can work from their homes. A signed agreement between the consultant and company representative will specify the work to be done and the amount of money to be paid.

Job Description

Management analysts and consultants are hired to collect specific information about a business. They study or analyze the information to solve the company's problems. They recommend the steps to take to solve problems. They take into account the general nature of the business, the internal organizational structure, and the relationship the business has with other businesses in that industry.

Working Conditions

Management analysts and consultants work in their offices and at the business of their clients. They may go to the production area to gather information. They often work more than 40 hours each week. The job may require frequent traveling.

Subjects to Study

Mathematics, English, speech, writing skills, computer skills, business, sciences

Discover More

Do you have a career interest that would enable you to be self-employed? Talk to someone you know who is self-employed. Find out what this person likes and dislikes about being self-employed. Compare the advantages and disadvantages.

Related Jobs

Managers, computer system analysts, operations research analysts, economists, financial analysts

Earnings	Education and Training	Job Outlook

High	Master's	Increasing rapidly

Marketing, Advertising, and Public Relations Managers

Job Description

Marketing, advertising, and public relations managers help businesses sell their products at a profit. Marketing managers decide who might buy the product and what new products might sell. Advertising managers decide what type of advertising will sell the most products. Public relations managers plan ways for businesses to get good public attention.

Working Conditions

Marketing, advertising, and public relations managers work in offices. Long hours including evenings and weekends are common. Working under pressure is unavoidable. These managers travel a lot, and job transfers are common.

Something Extra

Businesses do not want to be involved in controversy because it is not good for their public image. For example, a "Save the Animals" group might protest the sale of animal furs at a department store. The group might picket the store. To avoid embarrassment and inconvenience to its customers, the department store might stop selling furs.

Subjects to Study

Mathematics, English, speech, writing skills, journalism, business, economics, accounting

Discover More

Study commercials on television and radio. Read advertisements in newspapers and magazines. What do you notice about them? Create a poster to advertise a school event.

Related Jobs

Art directors, commercial and graphic artists, copy chiefs, copywriters, editors, lobbyists, marketing research analysts, public relations specialists, sales representatives, technical writers

Earnings	Education and Training	Job Outlook
High	Bachelor's	Increasing

Personnel, Training, and Labor Relations Specialists and Managers

Job Description

Personnel, training, and labor relations specialists and managers find the best employees for various jobs in a company. They must know employment laws and personnel policies to be able to discuss wages, working conditions, and promotion opportunities. They also train employees to work more efficiently. These people administer employee benefits, claims, health insurance, and retirement plans.

Something Extra

On-the-job training is one way many workers move to higher, better-paying jobs. Some companies have separate training facilities for this. Others train employees at the workplace. Large corporations may have schools with shops resembling the actual workplace where employees can train in pretend situations before actually starting work.

Working Conditions

Personnel, training, and labor relations specialists and managers work in offices. A 35- to 40-hour week is normal, but longer hours are sometimes necessary. Travel may be part of the job.

Subjects to Study

Mathematics, English, writing skills, speech, psychology, sociology, business, computer skills, economics, statistics

Discover More

Get a job application from a personnel office. What kind of information does a personnel manager look at when hiring employees? If you filled out the application, would you create a favorable impression on the personnel manager?

Related Jobs

Employment, rehabilitation, and college career planning and placement counselors, lawyers, psychologists, sociologists, social workers, public relations specialists, teachers

Earnings	Education and Training	Job Outlook

High	Bachelor's	Increasing

Property and Real Estate Managers

Job Description

Property and real estate managers are in charge of apartment buildings, businesses, and shopping malls. They sell empty space to renters. They prepare leases, collect rent, and handle the bookkeeping. They make sure that the property is maintained and handle complaints from renters.

Working Conditions

Property and real estate managers have offices, but much of their time is spent checking on properties. Evening meetings are common. They may have to live in an apartment complex to respond to emergencies and be on call 24 hours a day. Some real estate managers travel frequently.

Something Extra

In a few years you may be ready to move into an apartment. Before moving in you must sign a lease. A lease is an agreement between the renter and the property owner. It states the rent amount and the date of payment. Both the renter's and owner's responsibilities for apartment maintenance will be in the lease. Read it carefully!

Subjects to Study

Mathematics, English, writing skills, speech, business, accounting

Discover More

Talk to an apartment manager or landlord. Ask about the problems he or she experienced in the last month. What is the best part of this job? What is the worst part? What is your impression of a landlord?

Related Jobs

Restaurant and food service managers, hotel and resort managers and assistants, health services managers, education administrators, city managers

Earnings	Education and Training	Job Outlook
Low	Bachelor's	Increasing

Purchasers and Buyers

Something Extra

Supply is the amount of a product or service available. Demand is the price that people are willing to pay for that product. Supply and demand determine the prices for products and services. For example, lettuce costs 99 cents. In California, floods destroyed the lettuce crop. A few weeks later, lettuce cost $1.89. If supply is small, the prices go up. But if demand is small, the prices usually go down.

Job Description

Purchasers and buyers try to buy the best products for the lowest prices for their employers by negotiating the price with suppliers. They must be constantly aware of any changes that may affect the supply or demand of the products they purchase. They ensure that the right product amount is delivered at the right time.

Working Conditions

Purchasers and buyers work in comfortable offices. Working more than 40 hours a week is common, as is evening and weekend work. The time between Thanksgiving and early January may be so busy that vacations are discouraged. Traveling is usually required. Some purchasers may travel outside the United States.

Subjects to Study

Mathematics, English, speech, business, economics

Discover More

Read the newspaper grocery ads. Check the produce prices. Which vegetables and fruits are featured? Are the same vegetables and fruits available at the same prices at different stores? Why can some fruits and vegetables sell at lower prices?

Related Jobs

Retail sales workers, sales managers, comparison shoppers, manufacturers' and wholesale sales representatives, procurement services managers, traffic managers

Earnings	Education and Training	Job Outlook

Average	Bachelor's	Little change

Restaurant and Food Service Managers

Job Description

Restaurant and food service managers select food and establish prices. They check the quality of the food served and the service provided. These managers estimate food consumption and place orders so fresh food is delivered on a regular basis. They also place orders for kitchen and dining room supplies, hire and train workers, and do bookkeeping.

Working Conditions

Restaurant managers work nights and weekends regularly. The job can be hectic during the peak dining hours. Food service managers may work weekdays and daytime hours. Working 50 hours or more a week is common. Moving to a different city or state is often required.

Something Extra

Many restaurant chains require managers to attend rigorous training programs before starting their duties. Certain chains may teach trainees secret recipes and specific ways of providing service. The training also includes learning about nutrition, food preparation, cleanliness, security, and recordkeeping.

Subjects to Study

Mathematics, English, speech, business, nutrition, home economics courses, psychology

Discover More

When you eat at a restaurant, observe the methods used to serve the food quickly. What is the manager doing? When you go out to a different place, make the same observations. Compare the two places. Was the service the same? Was the food quality different? If you were manager, what changes would you make?

Related Jobs

Hotel managers and assistants, health services administrators, retail store managers, bank managers

Earnings	Education and Training	Job Outlook
Low	Associate/Bachelor's	Increasing rapidly

Retail Managers

Job Description

Retail managers sell goods and services directly to customers. They hire and schedule workers; order and price items; coordinate displays, ads, and sales announcements; and monitor profits, losses, and sales activity. These managers are responsible for complete customer satisfaction including handling complaints, answering questions, and ensuring that customers get prompt service and quality goods.

Something Extra

Young people are important customers to many retail businesses. They purchase clothing, sports equipment, CDs, and electronic equipment. As a customer, you should expect reasonable service and products —no matter what your age. Don't be afraid to talk to the manager if you don't get the treatment you expect.

Working Conditions

Most retail managers work in an office and in the store. Working more than 40 hours a week is common during busy shopping seasons. Evening and weekend work is expected. Working hours can change from week to week. Higher level managers travel often.

Subjects to Study

Mathematics, English, speech, psychology, sociology, business, accounting, computer skills

Discover More

Take a survey of friends and relatives. Ask them where they shop for clothing and why. Ask them if they have ever returned items to those stores. How did that experience affect their attitude about the store? Are they still satisfied customers?

Related Jobs

Managers in wholesale trade, hotels, banks, hospitals, law firms

Earnings	Education and Training	Job Outlook

Low	Associate/Bachelor's	Little change

Underwriters

Job Description

Underwriters work for insurance companies. They decide if a person applying for insurance is a good risk. They review insurance applications, medical reports, and other reports to make these decisions. Underwriters may help or hinder the profit an insurance company makes.

Working Conditions

Underwriters work in comfortable offices. A normal work week is 35 to 40 hours. Some overtime may be required. Underwriters may occasionally attend meetings away from home for a few days. Some may travel to work sites to assess risks.

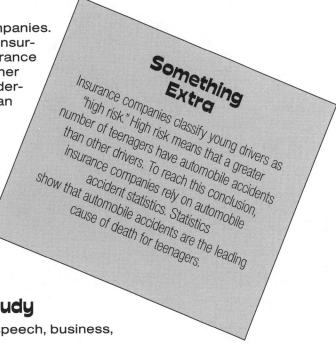

Something Extra

Insurance companies classify young drivers as "high risk." High risk means that a greater number of teenagers have automobile accidents than other drivers. To reach this conclusion, insurance companies rely on automobile accident statistics. Statistics show that automobile accidents are the leading cause of death for teenagers.

Subjects to Study

Mathematics, English, writing skills, speech, business, accounting, economics

Discover More

Ask your parents how much they pay for auto insurance. Find out how much more the auto insurance costs if you become a driver. Your parents' insurance agent is a good source for this information. Ask if you qualify for a "good student" price discount.

Related Jobs

Budget analysts, financial advisors, loan officers, credit managers, real estate appraisers, risk managers

Earnings	Education and Training	Job Outlook
Average	Bachelor's	Little change

Professional Specialty Occupations

Engineers

Job Description

Engineers may work in a wide variety of areas. Engineers design machinery, construct buildings and highways, and develop new products and new methods of making products. Some engineers test the quality of products. Some supervise the production in factories.

Working Conditions

Engineers work in laboratories, industrial plants, and offices. Others work at construction sites, where they inspect, supervise, or solve onsight problems. Some work outside part of the time. A 40-hour week is normal, but deadlines may mean longer hours and added stress.

Subjects to Study

Mathematics, English, physical sciences, physics, chemistry, technology courses, computer skills

Discover More

Talk to someone who is an engineer. Where did this person attend school? What special area of engineering does this person use? Where does this person work? Has this person worked as part of an engineering team?

Related Jobs

Physical scientists, life scientists, computer scientists, mathematicians, engineering and science technicians, architects

Earnings	Education and Training	Job Outlook

Average	Bachelor's	Little change

Aerospace Engineers

Job Description

Aerospace engineers design and test aircraft, missiles, and spacecraft. They develop new technology in aviation, defense systems, and space exploration. They may specialize in a certain type of craft, such as helicopters, spacecraft, or rockets.

Working Conditions

Many aerospace engineers work for companies that make aircraft, missiles, and space vehicles. States such as Texas, California, and Washington have large aerospace manufacturing industries. These engineers work 40 hours each week, but may have deadlines that require extra working time. Federal government agencies provide more than 1 out of 10 jobs in this field.

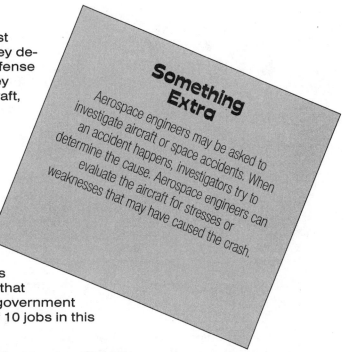

Something Extra

Aerospace engineers may be asked to investigate aircraft or space accidents. When an accident happens, investigators try to determine the cause. Aerospace engineers can evaluate the aircraft for stresses or weaknesses that may have caused the crash.

Subjects to Study

Mathematics, physics, chemistry, computer technology, physical science, drafting, technological skills, social science, English

Discover More

Learn about aerospace engineering by experimenting. Build a model rocket. If a model rocket club is available in your community, you may want to join to learn even more.

Related Jobs

Scientists, mathematicians, engineering and science technicians, other types of engineers

Earnings	Education and Training	Job Outlook
Very high	Bachelor's	Decreasing

Chemical Engineers

Something Extra

The novel *Dr. Jekyll and Mr. Hyde*, written more than 100 years ago, tells the story of the effect of chemistry on the human body. When the good Dr. Jekyll drank the chemicals he produced in his laboratory, he became the evil Mr. Hyde. Unfortunately, even today good people do evil things when drugs become a part of their lifestyle.

Job Description

Chemical engineers use chemistry and engineering to help produce chemicals and chemical products. They design equipment, plan how to make the products, and supervise the production. They may work in pollution control.

Working Conditions

Chemical engineers usually work in laboratories or factories. They may work for electronics or aircraft manufacturing plants or in petroleum refining and related industries. Some work independently as consultants. They may be hired to help companies control pollution. A 40-hour work week is common.

Subjects to Study

Mathematics, physics, chemistry, biology, environmental science, computer science, technological skills, English

Discover More

With your parents' permission, try some chemical experiments. Check your science book from school. Many of the chemicals may be in your kitchen. Remember to read and follow the directions carefully. Don't just mix chemicals. The wrong mixture can have harmful results.

Related Jobs

Scientists, mathematicians, engineering and science technicians, architects, other engineers

Earnings	Education and Training	Job Outlook

Very high	Bachelor's	Little change

Civil Engineers

Job Description

Civil engineers design and supervise construction of roads, bridges, tunnels, airports, water and sewage systems, and buildings. Some civil engineers work in research or teach other engineers. Many hold managerial positions ranging from supervisor of a construction site to city engineer.

Working Conditions

Civil engineers work mainly in offices, but part of their work is done outdoors at building sites. A 40-hour week is normal. Often they work in large industrial cities, but some projects may be in very isolated places or in foreign countries. Civil engineers often move from place to place working on different projects. Many work for federal, state, and local government agencies.

Something Extra

Structures must be built in different ways in different parts of the world. In California and Japan, earthquakes are a constant threat. An engineer must plan construction with earthquakes in mind when designing a structure for these areas. States bordering the ocean, such as Florida and Texas, are in danger of being struck by hurricanes. Some newer buildings in these areas have hurricane safeguards built in.

Subjects to Study

Mathematics, physical sciences, drafting, computer science, technological skills, environmental science, geology, English, foreign languages

Discover More

Join a structure building team through your school. Check with the enrichment teacher or a science teacher to find out more about this activity.

Related Jobs

Scientists, mathematicians, engineering and science technicians, architects, other engineers

Earnings	Education and Training	Job Outlook
High	Bachelor's	Little change

Electrical and Electronics Engineers

Job Description

Electrical and electronics engineers design, develop, test, and supervise the making of electrical equipment. They also solve problems involved with using the equipment. This includes electric generators and motors, wiring in automobiles, computers, and video equipment. They determine how long a project will take and how much it will cost.

Working Conditions

Electrical and electronics engineers work mostly in manufacturing firms, although some work for utility companies, computer firms, and government agencies. They usually work 40-hour weeks, with some overtime required.

Subjects to Study

Mathematics, chemistry, physics, computer science, drafting, technological classes, English

Discover More

Ask someone who works with electrical equipment to show you the inside of a radio, VCR, or computer. What safety precautions are taken before the equipment is opened? Look at the wiring inside the equipment. Ask the individual to explain the wiring. Is there a diagram of the wiring inside the equipment?

Related Jobs

Scientists, mathematicians, engineering and science technicians, architects, other engineers

Earnings	Education and Training	Job Outlook
Very high	Bachelor's	 Little change

Industrial Engineers

Job Description

Industrial engineers find the most effective ways to use people, machines, and materials to make a product. Using mathematics, these problem solvers help the company make the best products for the least amount of money. They help find new factory locations with the best combinations of raw materials, transportation, and costs. They are the bridge between management and operations. Computers help them do faster work and save money.

Something Extra

Every manufacturer needs raw materials to make a product. For example, the Grandma's Rocking Chair Company needs wood to produce wooden rocking chairs. For that reason, an industrial engineer would advise the company to build its factory in a lumbering area rather than a desert area.

Working Conditions

Industrial engineers work mostly in offices of manufacturing industries. Some work for hospitals, banks, and other businesses. These engineers work more closely with people than other types of engineers.

Subjects to Study

Mathematics, computer science, physical sciences, drafting

Discover More

Learn to be a problem solver. Check the library for a book of mathematical puzzles. How many problems can you solve?

Related Jobs

Scientists, mathematicians, engineering and science technicians, architects, other engineers

Earnings	Education and Training	Job Outlook

High	Bachelor's	Little change

Mechanical Engineers

Job Description

Mechanical engineers design tools, engines, machines, and other mechanical equipment. Rocket engines, robots, and refrigerators are some of the products designed by mechanical engineers. These engineers also design tools that other engineers use in their work. Some mechanical engineers work in production operations, maintenance, and technical sales.

Working Conditions

Most mechanical engineers work for companies in the manufacturing industry. Most work 40 hours a week. They may work with other types of engineers in offices or factories. Computers are frequently used in their work.

Subjects to Study

Mathematics, physical science, drafting, computer science, technological skills

Discover More

Arrange a visit to an engineering school or a college that offers engineering classes. If you can tour the laboratory areas, you might see some robots in action.

Related Jobs

Scientists, mathematicians, engineering and science technicians, architects, other engineers

Earnings	Education and Training	Job Outlook

Very high	Bachelor's	Little change

Metallurgical, Ceramic, and Materials Engineers

Job Description

Metallurgical, ceramic, and materials engineers develop new kinds of metals, ceramics, and other materials to do special jobs. One example is the ceramic tiles on the space shuttle that prevent it from overheating. These engineers also study and test metals to make new products from them, such as the composite materials now being used in "stealth" aircraft. They find ways to make metals better, such as making a metal stronger without increasing its weight.

Something Extra

Ceramic tile can be found in the shower or bathtub in your house but it has also been used in outer space. The space shuttle is built using ceramic tiles. Without the protection of these tiles, the space shuttle would overheat and burn when it reenters the earth's atmosphere from its space flight.

Working Conditions

Metallurgical, ceramic, and materials engineers work indoors in industries. They normally work 40-hour weeks. Many of these workers must wear protective clothing and glasses when performing their daily duties.

Subjects to Study

Mathematics, chemistry, physics, drafting, English

Discover More

Gather a variety of materials—paper, metals, clay, tiles. Use your creative abilities. What useful product can you make?

Related Jobs

Scientists, mathematicians, engineering and science technicians, architects, other engineers

Earnings	Education and Training	Job Outlook
Average	Bachelor's	Increasing

Mining Engineers

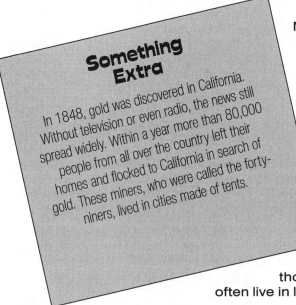

Something Extra

In 1848, gold was discovered in California. Without television or even radio, the news still spread widely. Within a year more than 80,000 people from all over the country left their homes and flocked to California in search of gold. These miners, who were called the forty-niners, lived in cities made of tents.

Job Description

Mining engineers find, remove, and prepare metals and minerals for industries. They are in charge of the safe construction of mines, tunnels, and open pits. They make sure that mines are safe for workers and the environment. Many specialize in the mining of one mineral such as gold or coal. Some work designing new mining equipment.

Working Conditions

Mining engineers work in offices and laboratories as well as outside. They frequently work and live in the area of the mine location, which is often near a small community. However, those in research, sales, or management often live in larger cities.

Subjects to Study

Mathematics, physics, geology, chemistry, environmental science, drafting, English

Discover More

Geology is the study of the earth and how it is formed. Study the rocks in your area. When you visit another part of the country, observe the differences between the rocks and soil at your home and the place you are visiting. You may want to start a rock collection.

Related Jobs

Scientists, mathematicians, engineering and science technicians, architects, other engineers

Earnings	Education and Training	Job Outlook

Average	Bachelor's	Little change

Nuclear Engineers

Job Description

Nuclear engineers study nuclear energy and radiation. They design and operate nuclear power plants which provide electricity and operate Navy ships. Others develop nuclear weapons or study uses of radiation in industry and medicine.

Working Conditions

Nuclear engineers work in laboratories and offices, although outdoor work may be required at times. Many are employed by the federal government. Because of the major safety concerns, this job is often stressful. Forty-hour work weeks are normal.

Something Extra

Meltdown is the most severe accident that can happen at a nuclear reactor. In a meltdown the radioactive material becomes so hot that it melts some or all of the fuel in the reactor. If the radioactive material gets into the environment, it is harmful to all living things—plants, animals, and people. Both the United States and the USSR have had destructive meltdowns in recent years.

Subjects to Study

Mathematics, physical sciences, chemistry, physics, drafting, biology, environmental studies

Discover More

To learn more about meltdown, ask a librarian for information about the partial meltdown at the Three Mile Island nuclear power plant in 1979 and the complete meltdown at Chernobyl in 1986.

Related Jobs

Scientists, mathematicians, engineering and science technicians, architects, other engineers

Earnings	Education and Training	Job Outlook

Average	Bachelor's	Little change

Petroleum Engineers

Job Description

Petroleum engineers explore for and produce oil and natural gas. They find the least expensive and most efficient ways to extract the oil and gas from the earth. Because only a small portion of oil and gas in a reservoir will flow out, they inject water, chemicals, or steam into the reservoir to force more out.

Working Conditions

Petroleum engineers work in laboratories, offices, and outdoors. Many work in states that have large amounts of fossil fuels, such as Texas, Oklahoma, Louisiana, and California. Some work in offshore drilling sites and some work as independent consultants. Many American petroleum engineers work in oil-producing countries in other parts of the world, such as Saudi Arabia.

Something Extra

Petroleum and natural gas are fossil fuels. They are produced from decaying plants and animals that have been buried underground for millions of years. Because of the vast amounts of time needed to produce oil and natural gas, they cannot be replaced quickly.

Subjects to Study

Mathematics, physical sciences, geology, chemistry, physics, environmental studies, biology

Discover More

Oil and water don't mix. Try a fun experiment. Put 1/4 cup of vegetable oil in a clear plastic bottle. Fill the bottle with water and put the lid on securely. Shake the bottle and watch the results. For variety, put food coloring or glitter in the bottle.

Related Jobs

Scientists, mathematicians, engineering and science technicians, architects, other engineers

Earnings	Education and Training	Job Outlook

Average	Bachelor's	Decreasing

Architects

Job Description

Architects design buildings and other structures. They make sure that these buildings are functional, safe, and economical. Architects meet with their clients to learn the needs of the people who will use the building. Architects draw plans of every part of a building, including plumbing and electrical systems. They also help choose a building site and the construction materials.

Working Conditions

Architects spend most of their time in offices talking with clients, writing reports, and making designs. Although architects worked with pencil and paper in the past, most now use computers for drawing. Much of their work is done with other architects and engineers, sometimes on the construction site. A 40-hour week is normal. Deadlines may mean working nights and weekends.

Something Extra

Thomas Jefferson, the third president of the United States, had many talents, including architecture. Jefferson designed his famous house in Virginia called Monticello. He also planned the campus of the University of Virginia. The Capitol building in Washington, D.C., is another structure that Jefferson created.

Subjects to Study

Mathematics, English, writing skills, communication skills, drawing courses, drafting, computer skills

Discover More

Observe houses in your community. Think about the features you like in other people's homes. Draw a room-by-room floor plan of your dream home.

Related Jobs

Landscape architects, building contractors, civil engineers, urban planners, interior designers, industrial designers, drafters, graphic designers.

Earnings	Education and Training	Job Outlook
High	Professional degree	Little change

Landscape Architects

Job Description

Landscape architects make areas such as parks, campuses, malls, and golf courses beautiful and useful. They plan the location of buildings, roads, and walkways and the arrangement of flowers and trees. Natural resource conservation and historic preservation are important in their planning.

Working Conditions

Landscape architects work in offices and at landscaping sites. They create designs, estimate costs, and check that the plans are being done correctly. Most work regular 40-hour weeks. Some landscape architects are self-employed.

Subjects to Study

Mathematics, English, botany, ecology, drafting, art courses, geology, physical sciences, social sciences

Discover More

Attend a program conducted by a master gardener. A master gardener is someone in your community who is an expert at gardening. He or she belongs to a group of interested persons who promote the importance of plants to the earth's ecology. To find out about these programs, contact a garden club or botanical garden.

Related Jobs

Architects, interior designers, civil engineers, urban and regional planners, botanists, horticulturists

Earnings	Education and Training	Job Outlook

High	Bachelor's	Little change

Surveyors

Job Description

Surveyors measure and map the earth's surface. Land surveyors set official land, air, space, and water boundaries. They plan the work, check old legal documents for information, and write reports for legal documents. They are the chief of a survey party. A survey technician operates the survey instruments and records the measurements. Mapping scientists use the information they gather to prepare maps and charts.

Something Extra

Satellites are changing the way surveying is done. The Global Positioning System is a satellite system that uses radio signals from satellites to locate points on the earth. A radio receiver about the size of a backpack is placed at the desired point. Information is collected from several satellites at once. A receiver can be placed in a vehicle to trace a road system.

Working Conditions

Surveyors work outdoors doing very active work. They work in all types of weather and may travel to work sites. They work eight-hour days, five days each week. Summer hours may be longer. Some surveyors work in offices.

Subjects to Study

Algebra, geometry, trigonometry, drafting, mechanical drawing, computer science, English, writing skills, geography, geology, physical science, computer skills

Discover More

Look at different types of maps. Atlases, road maps, and magazines such as *National Geographic* are excellent sources of map learning. Use a map to travel to familiar and new places.

Related Jobs

Civil engineers, architects, geologists, geophysicists, geographers, urban planners

Earnings	Education and Training	Job Outlook
Average	Bachelor's	Little change

Actuaries

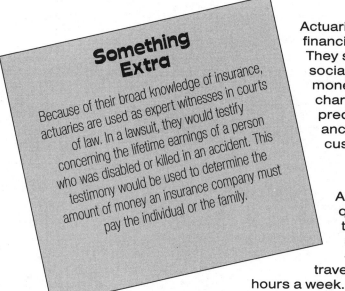

Something Extra

Because of their broad knowledge of insurance, actuaries are used as expert witnesses in courts of law. In a lawsuit, they would testify concerning the lifetime earnings of a person who was disabled or killed in an accident. This testimony would be used to determine the amount of money an insurance company must pay the individual or the family.

Job Description

Actuaries design insurance plans that are financially sound and help make a profit. They study statistics, economics, and social trends to determine the amount of money an insurance company should charge for an insurance policy. They predict the amount of money an insurance company will pay to its customers for claims.

Working Conditions

Actuaries have desk jobs that require no unusual physical activity; their offices are generally comfortable and pleasant. Most work a 40-hour week. Consulting actuaries travel often and may work more than 40 hours a week.

Subjects to Study

Mathematics, calculus, accounting, computer science, English, communication skills

Discover More

Ask your parents how much they pay for automobile insurance. Find out how much their auto insurance costs will change when you start to drive. Why do young drivers pay more for auto insurance than older drivers?

Related Jobs

Accountants, economists, financial analysts, mathematicians, rate analysts, rate engineers, risk managers, statisticians, value engineers

Earnings	Education and Training	Job Outlook

Average	Bachelor's	Increasing

Computer Scientists and Systems Analysts

Job Description

Computer scientists conduct research, design computers, and find new ways to use computers. Systems analysts identify problems in business, science, and engineering. They use computers to solve these problems.

Working Conditions

Computer scientists and systems analysts work in offices and laboratories. A 40-hour week is common, with occasional evening or weekend work. The large amount of computer work involved in this job can result in eye strain, back discomfort, and hand and wrist problems.

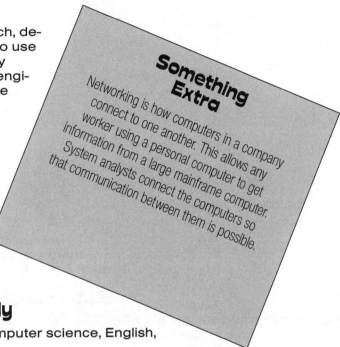

Something Extra

Networking is how computers in a company connect to one another. This allows any worker using a personal computer to get information from a large mainframe computer. System analysts connect the computers so that communication between them is possible.

Subjects to Study

Mathematics, physical sciences, computer science, English, communication skills

Discover More

Visit a computer store. Explore the various types of computers. Notice how they can be operated—keyboard, touch pad, mouse. Check out the software available to computer users.

Related Jobs

Computer programmers, financial analysts, urban planners, engineers, operations research analysts, management analysts, actuaries

Earnings	Education and Training	Job Outlook
High	Bachelor's	Increasing rapidly

Mathematicians

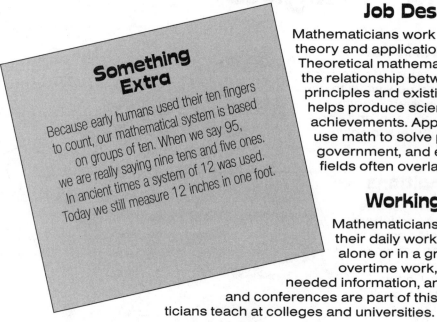

Something Extra

Because early humans used their ten fingers to count, our mathematical system is based on groups of ten. When we say 95, we are really saying nine tens and five ones. In ancient times a system of 12 was used. Today we still measure 12 inches in one foot.

Job Description

Mathematicians work in the areas of theory and applications of mathematics. Theoretical mathematicians work with the relationship between new math principles and existing ones. This work helps produce scientific and engineering achievements. Applied mathematicians use math to solve problems in business, government, and everyday life. The two fields often overlap.

Working Conditions

Mathematicians use computers in their daily work. They may work alone or in a group. Deadlines, overtime work, requests for special needed information, and travel to seminars and conferences are part of this job. Many mathematicians teach at colleges and universities.

Subjects to Study

Mathematics, algebra, geometry, trigonometry, calculus, logic, computer science, physical science, English, communication skills

Discover More

Have you looked at your watch today? Have you bought anything? Every day you use mathematics. Make a list of the ways you use numbers this week. You may be surprised at how long the list becomes.

Related Jobs

Actuaries, statisticians, computer programmers

Earnings	Education and Training	Job Outlook

Average	Bachelor's	Little change

Operations Research Analysts

Job Description

Operations research analysts help organizations operate in the most efficient way by applying scientific and mathematical principles to problems. First, they define and study the problem. Next, they gather information about each part of the problem by talking with various people and selecting a model to be used to solve the problem. Finally, the analyst's findings and recommendations are presented to the organization's management.

Working Conditions

Operations research analysts work regular hours in an office environment. They often work under pressure on projects that have deadlines and may work more than a 40-hour week.

Something Extra

To operate effectively, an airline must schedule flights at times that meet its passengers' needs. An operations research analyst coordinates the flight schedule and maintenance work, estimates the number of passengers flying at different times, and determines the amount of fuel needed for each flight. With this information, the analyst produces a schedule that provides safe flights while making money for the airline.

Subjects to Study

Mathematics, computer skills, English, communication skills, logic

Discover More

Learning how to solve problems is an important life skill. Think of a problem that your class or family faces. Explore all of the different parts of the problem. Talk to other members of your class or family to find out their opinions. Select a solution and try it out.

Related Jobs

Computer scientists, applied mathematicians, statisticians, economists, managerial occupations

Earnings	Education and Training	Job Outlook
High	Master's	Increasing rapidly

Statisticians

Something Extra

A doctor prescribes a new drug to a patient. Does the drug have any side effects? Is the patient sleeping well? Is the patient experiencing any emotional stress? A survey of patients can answer these questions. A statistician can offer this information about the drug's safety and effectiveness to the company that produces it.

Job Description

Statisticians design, collect, and use data from surveys and experiments. They decide where and how to gather data, who will be surveyed, and what questions will be asked. The information collected helps them make predictions concerning growth or the economy or assess various social problems. This helps business and government leaders make decisions.

Working Conditions

Statisticians normally work regular hours in offices. Some travel occasionally to set up a survey or gather data. Some may have repetitious tasks, while others have a variety of duties.

Subjects to Study

Mathematics, algebra, statistics, economics, business, sciences, English, computer skills, communication skills

Discover More

Telemarketing—calling people on the phone—is one way surveys are conducted. Check the want ads of the newspaper for ads hiring telemarketers. Can you tell which ones need people to sell a product and which ones need workers to gather research information?

Related Jobs

Actuaries, mathematicians, operations research analysts, computer programmers, computer systems analysts, engineers, economists, financial analysts, information scientists, life scientists, physical scientists, social scientists

Earnings	Education and Training	Job Outlook

High	Bachelor's	Little change

Agricultural Scientists

Job Description

Agricultural scientists study farm crops and animals to improve their quantity and quality. They look for ways to control pests and weeds safely, increase crop yields with less labor, and save water and soil. They research ways to make healthy, attractive food products for consumers. Agricultural scientists specialize in the areas of food, plant, soil, or animal science.

Working Conditions

Agricultural scientists who are managers or researchers work regular hours in offices and laboratories. Many agricultural scientists work outdoors. Food scientists may work in test kitchens. Animal scientists may work in dairies or on farms.

Something Extra

Will chickens hatch in outer space? Scientists wondered if the lack of gravity would have an effect on hatching eggs. An agricultural scientist sent fertilized chicken eggs into space aboard the space shuttle. Some of the eggs did not survive the flight. Of the eggs that survived, some did hatch. The baby space chickens returned to Earth to be studied further.

Subjects to Study

English, communication skills, mathematics, economics, business, physical sciences, life sciences, nutrition

Discover More

Plants grow in many different ways. Some require lots of water and little sunlight, others need lots of sunlight and little water. Try growing some plants of your own. A plant book will help you learn how to care for different kinds of plants.

Related Jobs

Chemists, physicists, farmers, farm managers, cooperative extension service agents, foresters, conservation scientists, veterinarians, horticulturists, landscape architects, soil scientists, soil conservationists

Earnings	Education and Training	Job Outlook
High	 Bachelor's/Master's	 Little change

Biological and Medical Scientists

Something Extra

Smoking greatly increases the risk of lung cancer. Medical scientists have proven through numerous studies and experiments that this statement is true. Supplying and explaining facts to the public is one way medical scientists help people prevent health problems and live longer, healthier lives.

Job Description

Biological and medical scientists study living things and their relationship to their environment. They do research, develop new medicines, increase crop amounts, and improve the environment. They study specialty areas such as ocean life, plant life, or animal life.

Working Conditions

Biological and medical scientists work regular hours in offices and laboratories. Medical scientists may work in clinics or hospitals. Some travel to primitive places to do research. In the lab, safety is important because dangerous or toxic substances may be present.

Subjects to Study

Mathematics, English, biology, botany, chemistry, physics, communication skills, computer skills

Discover More

Ask your family doctor about research that he or she may have been involved in during medical school.

Related Jobs

Foresters, range managers, soil conservationists, animal breeders, horticulturists, soil scientists, other agricultural scientists, life science technicians, medical doctors, dentists, veterinarians

Earnings	Education and Training	Job Outlook

Very high	Master's/Doctorate	Increasing

Foresters and Conservation Scientists

Job Description

Foresters and conservation scientists manage, use, and protect natural resources such as water, wood, and wildlife. Foresters supervise the use of timber for lumbering. Range managers manage, improve, and protect rangelands without damaging the environment. Soil conservationists help farmers save the soil, water, and other natural resources.

Working Conditions

Working conditions for foresters and conservation scientists are varied. Some work alone while others deal with the public every day. Some work regular hours in offices or labs, but others work outdoors in all kinds of weather. When emergencies such as a fire occur, long hours of work are necessary.

Something Extra

Aerial photographs—pictures taken from airplanes or satellites—are very useful to foresters in mapping forests and studying the use of land and forests. These photographs show widespread trends in the forest, such as where certain types of trees may be growing or where vegetation is dying. Through their use foresters are able to see the big picture.

Subjects to Study

Mathematics, science, communication skills, computer science, economics, business, ecology, biology, agriculture

Discover More

Visit a state or national park or preserve in your area. What natural resources do you find there? Water? Wood? Sand? Minerals? Check the library for magazines about your state and its natural resources.

Related Jobs

Agricultural scientists, agricultural engineers, biological scientists, environmental scientists, farmers, farm managers, ranchers, ranch managers, soil scientists, soil conservation technicians, wildlife managers

Earnings	Education and Training	Job Outlook
Low	Bachelor's	Little change

Chemists

Something Extra

Not all chemicals are harmful or artificial. All physical things, whether found naturally or created by humans, are made of chemicals. You can create a chemical reaction by mixing two simple ingredients found in your kitchen—baking soda and vinegar. A gas is produced by the chemical reaction.

Job Description

Chemists look for and use new information about chemicals. They develop new paints, fibers, adhesives, drugs, and other products. They develop processes that save energy and reduce pollution. They make improvements in such areas as agriculture, medicine, and food processing.

Working Conditions

Chemists work regular hours in offices and labs. The majority are employed in manufacturing firms. Some work for government agencies or teach at colleges and universities. Some research may be done in chemical plants or outdoors. Chemists must take safety precautions when handling certain dangerous chemicals.

Subjects to Study

Mathematics, physical sciences, physics, chemistry, biology, computer science, English, business

Discover More

Find out more about being a chemist by writing for information to: American Chemical Society, Career Services, 1155 16th St. NW, Washington, D.C. 20036.

Related Jobs

Chemical engineers, agricultural scientists, biological scientists, chemical technicians, physical and life scientists

Earnings	Education and Training	Job Outlook

Average	Bachelor's	Little change

Geologists and Geophysicists

Job Description

Geologists and geophysicists study the history and physical aspects of the earth. They study rocks, collect information using sensing instruments in satellites, and construct maps. Many search for oil, natural gas, minerals, and underground water. They play an important role in cleaning up the earth's environment, designing waste disposal sites and reclaiming contaminated land and water.

Something Extra

Geologists and geophysicists study different areas of the earth. Geologists study the earth's crust. They try to find out how rocks were formed and what has happened since their formation. Geophysicists study both the earth's surface and what is inside the earth. Both scientists search for natural resources such as oil and gas and try to solve environmental problems.

Working Conditions

Geologists and geophysicists work outdoors and in offices and laboratories. One in four is employed by an oil or gas company. They may travel to remote areas or overseas. Job relocation is common.

Subjects to Study

Mathematics, computer science, chemistry, physics, geology, English

Discover More

Ask a science teacher about a geological formation in your area, such as a cave or mountain. Visit a natural history museum or a nature center at a state park to learn more about geology.

Related Jobs

Engineering technicians, science technicians, petroleum engineers, surveyors, some life scientists, physicists, chemists, meteorologists, mathematicians, computer scientists, soil scientists, mapping scientists

Earnings	Education and Training	Job Outlook

Average	Master's	Little change

Meteorologists

Something Extra

Weather balloons are used by meteorologists to measure wind, temperature, and humidity in the atmosphere. These balloons, launched twice each day, are supplemented by more complex instruments that supply information every few minutes. These instruments, such as Doppler radar, help forecasters better predict thunderstorms, flash floods, and tornadoes.

Job Description

Meteorologists study the atmosphere—the air that covers the earth—for its effects on our environment. The most well-known area of their work is weather forecasting. Meteorologists also conduct research and study trends in the earth's climate and apply their research to air-pollution control, agriculture, air and sea transportation, and defense.

Working Conditions

Meteorologists often work nights, weekends, and holidays at weather stations. Rotating shifts are worked to keep the stations open 24 hours a day, seven days a week. Weather forecasters are under pressure to get the weather report ready by a deadline. Those who are not forecasters work regular hours in offices.

Subjects to Study

Mathematics, English, chemistry, physics, physical science

Discover More

Listen to the weather forecast on television. Observe the equipment used by the forecaster. Listen for terms like humidity, barometric pressure, and Doppler radar. Read a book on weather and find out what these terms mean.

Related Jobs

Oceanographers, geologists, geophysicists, hydrologists, civil and environmental engineers

Earnings	Education and Training	Job Outlook

Average	Bachelor's	Little change

Physicists and Astronomers

Job Description

Physicists explore the structure and behavior of matter and forces of nature, such as gravity and nuclear interaction. They use their studies to develop medical equipment, electronic devices, and lasers. Astronomers study the universe, including the moon, sun, planets, and stars. Their knowledge is used in space flight and navigation. Both physicists and astronomers do large amounts of research.

Working Conditions

Physicists work regular hours in laboratories and offices. However, research may require irregular, long hours. Astronomers may travel to observatories in remote areas when night work is required.

Something Extra

The popular image of astronomers depicts them peering through a telescope at the heavens. Actually astronomers use enhanced photographs and electronic detecting equipment to make observations. These provide much better information than the human eye looking through a telescope can. Astronomers make observations only a few weeks each year; they spend most of their time doing research and writing scientific papers.

Subjects to Study

Mathematics, English, writing skills, physics, chemistry, communication skills, computer science

Discover More

A planetarium uses moving projectors to show stars, planets, and other heavenly bodies. Planetariums may be located on college campuses, at museums, or in some schools. Visit a planetarium. Learn about the universe.

Related Jobs

Chemists, geologists, geophysicists, mathematicians, engineers, engineering and science technicians

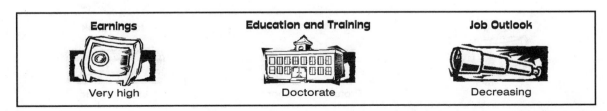

Earnings	Education and Training	Job Outlook
Very high	Doctorate	Decreasing

Lawyers and Judges

Job Description

Lawyers, also called attorneys, give people advice about the law and their rights. They represent people in court by presenting evidence that supports their client's position. Judges oversee trials and make sure that court rules are followed. In court cases without a jury, the judge decides the verdict.

Working Conditions

Lawyers and judges work in offices, law libraries, and courtrooms. A 50-hour week is common. Lawyers are often under stress when preparing for trial and may travel frequently. They spend time researching and reviewing other court cases, and must be skilled communicators.

Subjects to Study

English, writing skills, public speaking, government, history, foreign languages, economics, mathematics, computer science, logic

Discover More

Do you enjoy a stimulating argument? Join a debate team where you can learn how to present your argument logically. You will gain experience speaking before others and increase your self-confidence.

Related Jobs

Paralegal, arbitrator, journalist, patent agent, title examiner, legislative assistant, lobbyist, FBI special agent, political office holder, corporate executive

Earnings	Education and Training	Job Outlook

Very high	Professional degree	Little change

Social Scientists and Urban Planners

Job Description

Social scientists study all aspects of humans, including how people get the things they need, different religious beliefs, and mass transportation systems. They conduct surveys, study historic records, and do experiments with people and animals. Social scientists often study a special field, such as economics, history, politics, or groups. Urban planners study population growth and social and economic change to develop plans and programs for industrial and public sites.

Something Extra

During an election, political scientists supply voters with information about the candidates and political issues. They conduct public opinion polls, which ask voters questions about candidates and issues. This information is compiled and reported to the voting public. Many people believe that such polls influence other voters when they cast their votes.

Working Conditions

Most social scientists and urban planners work normal hours, although some regularly work overtime and must meet tight schedules and deadlines. Travel may be necessary.

Subjects to Study

Mathematics, English, speech, writing skills, computer science, statistics, psychology, economics, geography, history, foreign languages

Discover More

Genealogists trace family histories. To learn more about your family tree, talk to some of your older relatives—grandparents, great grandparents, great aunts and uncles. The library has many books to help you learn how to trace your family history.

Related Jobs

Lawyers, statisticians, mathematicians, computer programmers, computer scientists, systems analysts, reporters, correspondents, social workers, religious workers, college and university faculty, counselors

Earnings	Education and Training	Job Outlook

High-very high	Master's/Doctorate	Increasing

Economists and Marketing Research Analysts

Something Extra

Businesses expect a marketing research survey to be confidential. They do not want their competitors to know what information they are seeking or the results of the survey. For this reason, interviewers and office workers tabulating the results may not be told the client's name. Keeping business secrets is part of a marketing research analyst's job.

Job Description

Economists study how society uses resources such as land, labor, raw materials, and machinery to make products. They use their studies to advise businesses and government agencies about finance, labor, natural resources, and other areas. Marketing research analysts make recommendations to businesses about the best ways to sell a product based on information they gather through interviews and questionnaires.

Working Conditions

Economists and marketing research analysts may work alone or as part of a research team. Deadlines, overtime work, and tight schedules are part of this job. Travel may be necessary.

Subjects to Study

Mathematics, English, economics, business, statistics, computer science, psychology, accounting, foreign languages

Discover More

Check the business section of the newspaper. Read what economists say about the nation's economic future. Do all economists agree? What tools do economists use to predict the economic future?

Related Jobs

Financial managers, financial analysts, accountants and auditors, underwriters, actuaries, securities and financial services sales workers, credit analysts, loan officers, budget officers

Earnings	Education and Training	Job Outlook
High	Bachelor's	Little change

Psychologists

Job Description

Psychologists study the way people think, feel, and act, and work to understand, explain, and change people's behavior. Psychologists in applied fields may conduct training programs, do market research, or provide counseling. They may work with mentally or emotionally disturbed individuals. They work with schools, industries, and health institutions to help people deal with stress and changes in their lives such as divorce, physical disabilities, and aging.

Something Extra

Cognitive psychologists study the brain's role in memory, thinking, and understanding. In recent years, some have begun to use computer programming to create "artificial" intelligence. Artificial intelligence is created when a computer or robot is able to imitate human thought. A computer that can respond to a voice command appears to act almost human.

Working Conditions

Psychologists work in hospitals, schools, industries, and private offices. Some work standard 40-hour weeks; others work evenings and weekends. Those in private practice set their own hours. Traveling to attend conferences and conduct research is sometimes needed.

Subjects to Study

Mathematics, statistics, psychology, English, communication skills, biology, physical sciences, social sciences, computer science, writing skills

Discover More

Contact the mental health association in your community. Ask about any volunteer programs or projects they sponsor. Ask for information about careers in psychology.

Related Jobs

Psychiatrists, social workers, sociologists, clergy, special education teachers, counselors

Earnings	Education and Training	Job Outlook

Very high	Doctorate	Increasing rapidly

Sociologists

Something Extra

What is it like to be elderly? To find out, one young woman pretended to be old by changing her appearance. She then traveled to several different cities to test her experiment. Although she received some acts of kindness, her experiences mainly showed her that the elderly are often ignored or even treated abusively. Age has an effect on society's view of an individual.

Job Description

Sociologists observe families, communities, governments, and other organizations to learn about human behavior. They study how individuals are affected by each other and by the groups to which they belong. They examine the impact of people's gender, age, and race on their lives. They also research and evaluate social programs.

Working Conditions

Sociologists read, conduct research, and write reports, articles, and books. This mental work can be tiring and stressful as they cope with heavy workloads and deadlines. Knowing how to work as part of a team is important. Travel may be required for research projects or to attend conferences.

Subjects to Study

Mathematics, statistics, computer science, English, communication skills, psychology, sociology, writing skills, foreign languages

Discover More

Sociologists' and social workers' occupations are often confused. Talk to a social worker or a sociologist about the difference between them. Good sources of information are your school's social worker or a sociology teacher.

Related Jobs

Anthropologists, economists, geographers, historians, political scientists, psychologists, urban and regional planners, reporters and correspondents, social workers, intelligence specialists

Earnings	Education and Training	Job Outlook

High	Master's	Little change

Urban and Regional Planners

Job Description

Urban and regional planners develop programs that encourage growth in communities and regions. They devise plans for the best use of the land and study the area's schools, hospitals, parks, and other facilities to see if they meet the needs of the community. They also deal with legal codes and environmental issues.

Working Conditions

Urban and regional planners work mostly in offices but are sometimes outdoors examining land that is being developed. Evening and weekend meetings are common. Speaking at civic meetings and before legislative committees is part of this job. Pressures come from deadlines, tight work schedules, and groups opposed to land use proposals.

Something Extra

Computers help planners predict future trends such as population growth, housing and transportation needs, and employment. By using computerized geographic information systems, planners create overlay maps that can be changed to study different plans for the use of land. The computer-generated maps help planners visualize the effects of these changes.

Subjects to Study

Mathematics, English, public speaking, government, psychology, communication skills, writing skills, computer science

Discover More

Decisions about local planning are made by community councils and zoning boards. Check your newspaper for information about meetings of the town council or the county zoning board. Find out about zoning laws in your community.

Related Jobs

Architects, landscape architects, city managers, civil engineers, environmental engineers, geographers

Earnings	Education and Training	Job Outlook
Average	Bachelor's/Master's	Increasing

Human Services Workers

Job Description

Human services workers help clients who are disadvantaged in some way obtain benefits or services. They may direct projects such as food banks, train adults to live independently in society, or oversee adults who need assistance with daily tasks. They evaluate welfare clients' needs and their qualifications for government benefits, inform clients how to obtain services, monitor and keep case records on clients, and report progress to supervisors.

Something Extra

Human services workers belong to one of the fastest growing occupations in the United States. By the year 2005, the number of human services workers is expected to more than double. Major reasons for the growth include the increasing elderly population, the addition of more community-based programs, and the growing need for worker retraining as the economy grows.

Working Conditions

Human services workers work in offices, group homes, and the field. Workers may visit clients' homes or take clients to appointments. A 40-hour week is normal, but some night and weekend work may be required. The work, while rewarding, can be draining. As a result, worker turnover is high.

Subjects to Study

Mathematics, English, speech, psychology, sociology, writing skills

Discover More

Contact a local charitable organization. Volunteer to help at a food bank, an adult day-care center, or a mental health institution.

Related Jobs

Social workers, community outreach workers, religious workers, occupational therapy assistants, physical therapy assistants and aides, psychiatric aides, activity leaders

Earnings	Education and Training	Job Outlook

Very low-low	High school/Bachelor's	Increasing rapidly

Recreation Workers

Job Description

Recreation workers, such as camp counselors or coaches, organize leisure activities at parks, health clubs, camps, tourist attractions, and other places. They supervise the use and maintenance of recreational facilities and equipment. They teach people how to use equipment properly to avoid hurting themselves.

Working Conditions

Recreation workers work irregular hours, including nights and weekends. Their place of work may be a health club, a cruise ship, or a woodland park. Many recreation workers work part-time or seasonally. These workers do risk injury because of the physical activity in which they engage.

Something Extra

Some businesses send their executives to camp. At these adventure camps, recreation workers supervise the executives as they participate in activities in which they must depend on each other. Gliding down a rope high above the ground is one of the activities. The camps teach the executives to work together as a team.

Subjects to Study

Mathematics, English, communication skills, writing skills, business, accounting, physical education, swimming, art, music, drama, sports

Discover More

Volunteer to be a part of a recreational activity in your community. Volunteers are needed for activities such as community festivals, bicycle races, walkathons, and marathons.

Related Jobs

Recreational therapists, social workers, parole officers, human relations counselors, school counselors, clinical and counseling psychologists, teachers

Earnings	Education and Training	Job Outlook
Low	High school/Bachelor's	Increasing

Social Workers

Job Description

Social workers help people find solutions to their problems through counseling. They assist people in finding housing, jobs, and health care. Some of the problems they deal with include child and spouse abuse, teen pregnancy, alcohol and drug abuse, and criminal behavior. They also help people cope with serious illness, problem children, and aging parents.

Working Conditions

Social workers normally work a standard 40-hour week in offices, hospitals, or group homes. Those who offer counseling in private practice set their own hours. Weekend and night work is required at times to meet with clients or attend meetings. Pressure comes from understaffing and heavy caseloads. This job is satisfying, but can be emotionally draining.

Subjects to Study

Mathematics, English, writing skills, communication skills, psychology, biology, sociology, economics, history, foreign languages

Discover More

Make a list of social problems in your community, such as homelessness and child neglect. How are these problems being met? Are there organizations that assist people with their needs? Is help available through your school?

Related Jobs

Clergy, counselors, counseling psychologists, vocational rehabilitation counselors

Earnings	Education and Training	Job Outlook

Average	Bachelor's/Master's	Increasing

Protestant Ministers

Job Description

Protestant ministers are the leaders of their congregations. They write and give sermons, give encouragement and counseling to the sick, troubled, and grieving, and perform ceremonies and religious rites such as baptisms, marriages, and funerals. Many participate in community activities, as well. Some ministers are teachers in seminaries and colleges.

Something Extra

The education and training of Protestant ministers varies greatly. A denomination—a group of churches with the same beliefs—usually has its own school for training its ministers. Some churches require no formal training; others require both a bachelor's degree and a theological degree. Some independent churches form their own training schools, which are often called Bible colleges. Some allow women to become ministers, but others do not.

Working Conditions

The ministers of small congregations work personally with members, although ministers of large congregations have more administrative responsibilities and less contact with individuals. Ministers are on call for emergencies in their congregations' lives, and hours are often irregular and long. Much time is spent doing research and preparing sermons. Some ministers must move every few years.

Subjects to Study

English, writing skills, speech, history, sciences, social sciences, fine arts, music, foreign languages, mathematics

Discover More

Talk to a minister about this occupation. You might ask, Why did you choose to be a minister? What do you enjoy most about being a minister? What do you dislike about being a minister?

Related Jobs

Social workers, clinical and counseling psychologists, teachers, counselors

Earnings	Education and Training	Job Outlook

Average	High school/Bachelor's/Professional degree	Little change

Rabbis

Something Extra

There are four types of Jewish congregations: Orthodox, Conservative, Reform, and Reconstructionist. Although all types of congregations preserve basic Jewish worship, they differ in how they follow the traditional forms of worship. Some examples of these include the wearing of head coverings, speaking Hebrew when praying, and using traditional musical instruments or a choir during services.

Job Description

Rabbis are the spiritual leaders of their congregations, and teachers of Jewish law and tradition. They conduct religious services such as weddings and funerals and give sermons on the Sabbath and Jewish holidays. They offer comfort and counseling to the sick, grieving, and poor. Some rabbis teach in seminaries and colleges and write for religious publications. Many participate in community activities.

Working Conditions

Rabbis work long, irregular hours because they are on call for emergencies. They spend much time studying, researching, and writing sermons. Although they have a lot of independence in their work, rabbis report to a board of trustees from the congregation.

Subjects to Study

English, writing skills, speech, psychology, sciences, mathematics

Discover More

Talk to a rabbi about the education and work needed to become a rabbi. Find out the age that the rabbi chose this profession. What influenced this person to make this decision?

Related Jobs

Social workers, clinical and counseling psychologists, teachers, counselors

Earnings	Education and Training	Job Outlook

Average	Professional degree	Little change

Roman Catholic Priests

Job Description

Roman Catholic priests deliver sermons, distribute Holy Communion, and perform baptisms, weddings, and funerals. They comfort, counsel, and educate as needed. Priests must take a vow of poverty and agree to never marry. Diocesan priests serve the people of a diocese—a group of churches in an area. Religious priests are part of an order such as the Jesuits, Dominicans, or Franciscans. These priests may be missionaries or teachers. Some priests teach in high schools, colleges, or seminaries.

Something Extra

Currently, only men are allowed to serve as priests in the Roman Catholic church. This is a controversial issue for Catholics. Many feel that women should be allowed to become priests because they are permitted to serve in other church positions, including giving Holy Communion. As the shortage of priests increases, this issue will probably be debated even more in the Catholic church.

Working Conditions

Priests work long, irregular hours for the church and community. Diocesan priests are on call to serve in emergencies and often live in parish rectories. Other priests live in foreign countries as missionaries or in monasteries where they pray, study, and work.

Subjects to Study

English, speech, social studies, Latin, foreign languages, psychology, sociology

Discover More

Attend a Catholic church and observe a priest during mass. Talk to one and find out about the different types of priests. Ask about his education, work, and reasons for becoming a priest.

Related Jobs

Social workers, clinical and counseling psychologists, teachers, counselors

Earnings	Education and Training	Job Outlook

Average	Professional degree	Increasing

Adult Education Teachers

Job Description

Adult education teachers may teach skills to students who are updating their job skills or work with high school dropouts to prepare them to earn a high school diploma. Those who teach basic adult education may work with adults who do not speak English, or teach writing, reading, and mathematics to adults. Others teach courses such as floral arranging, cooking, or exercising to students who want to enrich their lives.

Something Extra

Illiteracy—the inability to read—is a secret that many adults hide for years. Amazingly, even some high school graduates are not able to read. Literacy programs have become very important in the United States in recent years, and many of these are available through local libraries. Volunteers in these programs teach adults how to read.

Working Conditions

Adult education teachers work mainly with motivated students who choose to be in class. As a result, behavior problems are not a part of the classroom, although some students do need help to develop study skills. Adult education teachers often work at night and on weekends because many students have jobs and families. Classes may last two to four hours, one day, or one semester.

Subjects to Study

English, communication skills, writing skills, mathematics, psychology, sciences, social sciences

Discover More

Go to a local community college and look at a catalog of the continuing education classes offered. Talk to a school counselor about how high school dropouts can earn a diploma. Ask your librarian about literacy programs.

Related Jobs

Other teachers, counselors, school administrators, public relations specialists, employee development specialists, interviewers, social workers

Earnings	Education and Training	Job Outlook

Average	Bachelor's/Master's	Little change

Archivists and Curators

Job Description

Archivists and curators are responsible for getting and preserving collections of value to the public. They plan exhibits, educational programs, and tours of the collections. These collections could consist of coins, stamps, paintings, animals, or other things. These items must be researched to ensure that they should be a part of the collection.

Working Conditions

Some archivists and curators work heavily with the public, providing educational services, while others work alone doing research or processing records. Physical activity may be required when restoring or installing exhibits. Curators travel to add to collections or organize exhibitions.

Something Extra

Archivists and curators do similar work. The major difference in their work is the items they collect. Curators work with three-dimensional objects, such as animals, plants, and sculptures. Archivists work mainly with records or objects that relate specifically to the records. These records may be saved on paper, film, or computer.

Subjects to Study

English, speech, history, art, chemistry, physics, business, mathematics

Discover More

Visit a museum or zoo. Observe the various exhibits and find out where the items were found and why they are included in the collection.

Related Jobs

Anthropologists, arborists, archaeologists, artifacts conservators, botanists, ethnologists, folklorists, genealogists, historians, horticulturists, information specialists, librarians, paintings restorers, records managers, zoologists

Earnings	Education and Training	Job Outlook

Average	Master's/Doctorate	Little change

College and University Faculty

Something Extra

Obtaining tenure, which ensures faculty jobs until they resign or retire, is a major reward in the academic world. Tenure is granted to professors who have worked for a university for several years and contributed to the school through their teaching and research. A committee of other professors judges their contributions. Tenure lets professors teach and conduct research without fear of being fired for introducing unpopular issues.

Job Description

College and university faculty teach, conduct large amounts of research, and serve on faculty committees. They stay aware of new developments in their field by reading, talking to colleagues, and attending conferences. They write scholarly articles and books about research they have done.

Working Conditions

College faculty work flexible schedules, but they must be present for classes and committee meetings. They may work staggered hours and teach night or weekend classes. Schedules are even more flexible during the summer when they can teach, do research, or travel. The pressure to do research in hopes of gaining tenure sometimes conflicts with the need to teach students.

Subjects to Study

English, mathematics, communication skills, writing skills, speech, sciences, social sciences, foreign languages, computer science

Discover More

Visit a college campus and attend a class. Observe the professor and think about how the class resembles and differs from your classes.

Related Jobs

Elementary and secondary school teachers, librarians, writers, consultants, lobbyists, trainers, employee development specialists, policy analysts, scientists, project managers, administrators in industry, government, and nonprofit research organizations

Earnings	Education and Training	Job Outlook

High	Doctorate	Little change

Counselors

Job Description

Counselors help people with their problems and concerns, but the type of work they do depends on the people they serve. School counselors help students with personal, social, and behavioral problems. College placement counselors help students and alumni with career development and job hunting. Rehabilitation counselors help people deal with their disabilities. Employment counselors help people make career decisions. Mental health counselors work to help their clients gain good mental health.

Something Extra

Counselors help people in times of crisis and tragedy. They may be called in to help people deal with the emotional effects of natural disasters such as tornadoes, earthquakes, and floods. Counselors also may be asked to help the loved ones of victims of tragedies such as airplane crashes.

Working Conditions

Counselors usually have private offices to allow their clients to talk freely. School counselors work the same hours as teachers, but other counselors normally work a 40-hour week. Some counselors work evenings to counsel clients who work during the day.

Subjects to Study

English, speech, psychology, mathematics, computer science, writing skills, communication skills

Discover More

Talk to your school counselor about this occupation. Find out about professional organizations that are available to counselors. Write to one of the organizations to learn more about counseling.

Related Jobs

College and student personnel workers, teachers, personnel workers and managers, human service workers, social workers, psychologists, psychiatrists, members of the clergy, occupational therapists, training and employment development specialists, equal opportunity/affirmative action specialists

Earnings	Education and Training	Job Outlook
Average	Master's	Increasing

Librarians

Job Description

Librarians manage staff, organize collections of library materials, and provide the public with information. User service librarians deal directly with the public to help them find information. Technical service librarians acquire and prepare materials for use. Administrative librarians manage the library by preparing budgets and supervising workers. Depending on the library, librarians may perform all or some of these duties.

Working Conditions

Librarians often spend all day at a desk or computer terminal, which may cause eyestrain or headaches. Their work can be busy and stressful at times. Some librarians work weekends or evenings, and one out of every four librarians works part-time.

Subjects to Study

English, mathematics, social sciences, sciences, business, computer science

Discover More

Check your local library for volunteer opportunities for young people. Also research a group called "Friends of the Library," which supports libraries in various ways.

Related Jobs

Archivists, information scientists, museum curators, publishers' representatives, research analysts, information brokers, records managers

Earnings	Education and Training	Job Outlook

Average	Professional degree	Little change

School Teachers/Kindergarten, Elementary, and Secondary

Job Description

Teachers help students learn by providing the tools and environment needed to develop their skills. Planning lessons, preparing tests, grading papers, and preparing reports of students' progress are part of a teacher's job. They meet with parents and school staff to discuss student progress and problems. Many also supervise extracurricular activities such as clubs and sports teams.

Something Extra

Keeping pace with technology is important in the world of teaching. Telecommunications technology can bring the real world into the classroom. For example, a class of American students can communicate with a class of Japanese students through the use of telecommunications. They can share personal experiences or research information that is of interest to both groups.

Working Conditions

Many teachers work more than 40 hours each week. Teachers on a 10-month schedule often spend their summer vacations attending college courses or workshops to continue their education. A year-round school schedule usually means eight weeks of classes with one week of vacation and a five-week winter break. Teaching is rewarding at times; however, dealing with unmotivated, badly behaved students can be stressful.

Subjects to Study

Mathematics, English, social sciences, sciences, foreign languages, computer science

Discover More

Check with your school counselor about programs such as peer tutoring or cadet teaching available in your school. Babysitting is another way to explore this job.

Related Jobs

College and university faculty, counselors, education administrators, employment interviewers, librarians, preschool workers, public relations specialists, sales representatives, social workers, trainers, employee development specialists

Earnings	Education and Training	Job Outlook

Average	Bachelor's	Increasing

Chiropractors

Something Extra

Holistic medicine, which emphasizes natural, drugless treatment, is used by chiropractors to help heal their patients. Holistic health recognizes that many factors affect a person's health. A chiropractor looks at the effect of a patient's environment and heredity on health as well as exercise, diet, and sleeping habits. A chiropractor may suggest lifestyle changes to patients to help them feel better.

Job Description

Chiropractors treat patients with health problems involving the muscles, nerves, and skeleton, especially the spine. They research patients' medical history, examine patients, order laboratory tests, and take X-rays. They do not prescribe drugs or perform surgery but emphasize nutrition, exercise, rest, and environment. Sometimes chiropractors manually manipulate or adjust the spinal column or use water, light massage, or heat therapy.

Working Conditions

Chiropractors work in clean, comfortable offices. Many are self-employed and set their own hours, but often work evenings and weekends to serve patients. Their average work week is 43 hours. Because they use X rays often, they must guard against dangers from radiation.

Subjects to Study

English, mathematics, health, biology, anatomy, nutrition, chemistry, physics, psychology, social sciences

Discover More

Contact the American Chiropractors Association, 1701 Clarendon Blvd., Arlington, VA 22209. Ask them to send you information about becoming a chiropractor.

Related Jobs

Physicians, dentists, optometrists, podiatrists, veterinarians, occupational therapists, physical therapists

Earnings	Education and Training	Job Outlook

Very high	Professional degree	Increasing

Dentists

Job Description

Dentists treat problems of the teeth and mouth tissue. They remove tooth decay, fill cavities, straighten teeth, and repair broken teeth. They also perform corrective surgery of the gums and supporting bones to treat gum disease. They offer instructions on how to brush, floss, and care for teeth to prevent problems. Some dentists, such as orthodontists, specialize in one particular area.

Something Extra

Wisdom teeth are the last teeth to emerge and are located behind the other teeth in the back of the mouth. Often they never grow above the gumline and must be removed to avoid infection that could affect other teeth. We call them "wisdom" teeth because they usually appear in the late teens or early twenties when people are more mature.

Working Conditions

Dentists work four or five days a week, 40 hours a week or more. Some work evenings and weekends to meet their patients' schedules. Many are self-employed. They wear masks, gloves, and safety glasses for protection from infectious diseases such as AIDS. Many dentists work part-time when they reach retirement age.

Subjects to Study

English, mathematics, communication skills, biology, anatomy, chemistry, physics, health, business

Discover More

Talk to your dentist about why he or she chose this occupation. Find out where your dentist went to school.

Related Jobs

Clinical psychologists, optometrists, physicians, chiropractors, veterinarians, podiatrists

Earnings	Education and Training	Job Outlook
Very high	Professional degree	Little change

Optometrists

Something Extra

Colorblindness is caused by a defect in certain cells in the retina, which is the inner layer of the eye. It occurs more frequently in men than women. Some people are partially colorblind. For example, they might not be able to see the difference between red and green. If a person is completely colorblind, all colors appear gray.

Job Description

Optometrists examine people's eyes to diagnose vision problems and eye diseases. They prescribe eyeglasses and contact lenses and may treat certain eye diseases. Some work in specialized areas, such as with the elderly or children. Others develop ways to protect workers' eyes from on-the-job strain or injury.

Working Conditions

Optometrists usually work in their own offices, which are clean, comfortable, and well-lighted. They work about 40 to 50 hours a week. They may work Saturdays and evenings to suit their patients' schedules.

Subjects to Study

English, mathematics, physics, chemistry, biology, psychology, history, sociology, speech, business

Discover More

To learn more about this occupation, have an eye examination or talk to someone who has had an examination. Have your optometrist explain the different tests that make up the examination and why each one is performed.

Related Jobs

Chiropractors, dentists, physicians, podiatrists, veterinarians, speech-language pathologists, audiologists

Earnings	Education and Training	Job Outlook

Very high	Professional degree	Little change

Physicians

Job Description

Physicians examine people who are suffering from illness or injury. They perform medical tests, prescribe and give treatment, and counsel people on health care. Most physicians specialize in one area of treatment such as diseases, allergies, or disorders. Those in private practice may oversee the business aspects of running an office.

Working Conditions

Physicians work long, irregular hours. Many work 60 hours a week or more. They may be on call for emergency visits to the hospital. Most physicians must travel frequently from their offices to hospitals to care for patients.

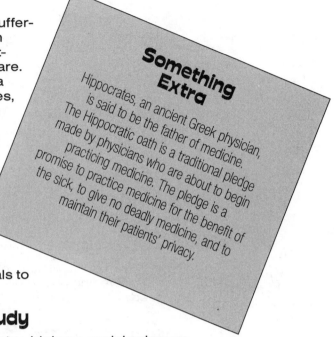

Something Extra

Hippocrates, an ancient Greek physician, is said to be the father of medicine. The Hippocratic oath is a traditional pledge made by physicians who are about to begin practicing medicine. The pledge is a promise to practice medicine for the benefit of the sick, to give no deadly medicine, and to maintain their patients' privacy.

Subjects to Study

English, mathematics, physics, chemistry, biology, social sciences, health

Discover More

Volunteering to work in a hospital or clinic will allow you to observe physicians as they perform their daily duties.

Related Jobs

Acupuncturists, audiologists, chiropractors, dentists, optometrists, podiatrists, speech pathologists, veterinarians

Earnings	Education and Training	Job Outlook
Very high	Professional degree	Increasing

Podiatrists

Something Extra

Twenty-six bones form the foot. Nerves, muscles, ligaments, and blood vessels are also a part of the foot. The foot provides a way of balancing the body, which is why tall people tend to have bigger feet than shorter people. Even the toes are important to our ability to walk and remain balanced. When someone loses a toe, therapy may be needed to help that person walk normally.

Job Description

Podiatrists diagnose and treat diseases, disorders, and injuries of the foot and lower leg. Podiatrists treat corns, calluses, ingrown toenails, bunions, heel spurs, and arch problems; ankle and foot injuries, deformities, and infections; and foot complaints caused by diseases such as diabetes. They prescribe medication and order physical therapy. They set broken bones and perform surgery.

Working Conditions

Podiatrists usually run their own small businesses. They spend time in their own offices or at the hospital visiting patients and performing surgery. Evening and weekend hours may be required to meet the needs of their patients.

Subjects to Study

English, mathematics, biology, chemistry, physics, business

Discover More

Write to the American Podiatric Medical Association, 9312 Old Georgetown Rd., Bethesda, MD 20814-1621. Ask for information about this occupation.

Related Jobs

Chiropractors, dentists, optometrists, physicians, veterinarians

Earnings	Education and Training	Job Outlook

Very high	Professional degree	Increasing

Veterinarians

Job Description

Veterinarians care for pets, farm animals, sporting and laboratory animals, and protect humans from diseases carried by animals. They set broken bones, dress wounds, prescribe medicine, perform surgery, and vaccinate animals against diseases. A number of veterinarians engage in research, food safety inspection, and education.

Working Conditions

Most veterinarians treat animals in private clinics or hospitals. Their facilities are often noisy, and they may be exposed to disease or infection through animal bites or scratches. Most veterinarians work 50 hours or more a week. They may work nights or weekends.

Something Extra

Some veterinarians specialize in the care of large animals such as horses and cows. They usually have an animal clinic on wheels, which they use to travel long distances to farms and ranches to treat their patients. Patients may need to be treated outdoors in all types of weather. The vet must beware of kicking, biting, and clawing patients.

Subjects to Study

English, mathematics, biology, chemistry, physics, business

Discover More

Visit a humane shelter. Talk to a worker about the responsibilities of pet owners. Find out what the humane society in your community is doing to help animals.

Related Jobs

Audiologists, chiropractors, dentists, optometrists, physicians, podiatrists, speech pathologists, animal trainers, zoologists, marine biologists, naturalists, veterinary technicians

Earnings	Education and Training	Job Outlook

Very high	Professional degree	Increasing

Dietitians and Nutritionists

Something Extra

Dietitians and nutritionists working with parents in home health care programs provide guidance in feeding infants and young children properly. For example, they may show parents how to prepare infant formula. They provide instructions on how to shop for groceries that are nutritious and help parents understand the need for healthy foods.

Job Description

Dietitians and nutritionists plan nutrition programs and supervise the preparation and serving of meals. They help prevent and treat illnesses by teaching clients to eat properly. Many decide the menus for institutions such as schools, nursing homes, and hospitals. Some clinical dietitians specialize in the management of overweight patients, care of the critically ill, or care of kidney or diabetic patients.

Working Conditions

Dietitians and nutritionists normally work 40-hour weeks. Some work weekends. Most work in pleasant areas, but spending time in a hot, steamy kitchen is possible. They may be on their feet much of the day.

Subjects to Study

English, mathematics, biology, chemistry, health, home economics, nutrition

Discover More

Talk to the person in charge of your school cafeteria. Ask what guidelines are followed in planning and preparing school lunches.

Related Jobs

Home economists, food service managers, nurses, health educators

Earnings	Education and Training	Job Outlook

Average	Bachelor's	Little change

Occupational Therapists

Job Description

Occupational therapists help people who have disabling conditions become independent and productive. Various activities are used to improve patients' skills. Therapists also help patients use adaptive equipment such as wheelchairs or splints. They may help patients find jobs and develop job skills. The ability to keep accurate records is important in this job.

Working Conditions

Occupational therapists normally work in hospitals, schools, or rehabilitation centers. Those providing home health care spend time driving to patients' homes. Most work a 40-hour week. This job can be tiring because workers spend a lot of time on their feet. Backstrain from lifting patients or moving equipment can be a problem.

Something Extra

Anorexia nervosa is an eating disorder. People with this problem, typically young females, refuse to eat and attempt to become extremely thin. The patient may die without medical help. Occupational therapists, counselors, and other medical workers help treat these patients.

Subjects to Study

Biology, chemistry, physics, health, art, social science, English, mathematics

Discover More

Read books about people who have overcome disabling conditions. Check the library for books about some of our presidents, sports heroes, and ordinary people who were able to succeed with the help of others.

Related Jobs

Orthotists, prosthetists, physical therapists, chiropractors, speech pathologists, audiologists, rehabilitation counselors, recreational therapists, art therapists, dance therapists, horticultural therapists, manual arts therapists

Earnings	Education and Training	Job Outlook
High	Bachelor's	Increasing

Pharmacists

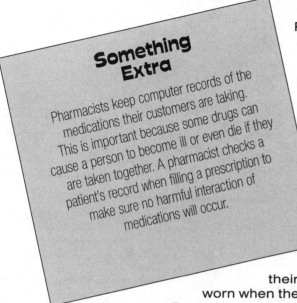

Something Extra

Pharmacists keep computer records of the medications their customers are taking. This is important because some drugs can cause a person to become ill or even die if they are taken together. A pharmacist checks a patient's record when filling a prescription to make sure no harmful interaction of medications will occur.

Job Description

Pharmacists dispense medication prescribed to people by their physician. They must know about the correct use, make-up, and effects of drugs. They answer questions patients ask about medication, including reactions or side effects that could occur from taking it. Pharmacists in hospitals and clinics advise the medical staff on the selection and effects of drugs, in some cases making rounds with them.

Working Conditions

Pharmacists usually work in clean, well-lighted areas in stores and hospitals. They must spend much of their workday standing. Gloves and masks are worn when they work with dangerous or sterile products. Evening, weekend, or holiday work is often required.

Subjects to Study

Mathematics, biology, chemistry, physics, social sciences, English

Discover More

Talk to a pharmacist at a drug store and ask about the training needed for this job. Ask how a pharmacist keeps up with new drugs that are developed.

Related Jobs

Pharmaceutical chemists, pharmacologists

Earnings	Education and Training	Job Outlook

High	Professional degree	Increasing

Physical Therapists

Job Description

Physical therapists work with accident victims and disabled individuals. They evaluate each patient's situation and write a plan to improve mobility, relieve pain, and limit permanent physical disabilities. These plans describe treatments, their purpose, and their intended effects. Physical therapists may use electricity, heat, or cold to relieve pain, reduce swelling, or increase flexibility.

Working Conditions

Physical therapists work in hospitals, clinics, and private offices with special equipment. They may treat patients in hospital rooms, schools, or homes. They work 40 hours a week, including some evenings and weekends. This job is physically demanding because equipment and patients need to be moved.

Something Extra

Passive exercise is one way that physical therapists help patients who have been unable to move for a period of time. The therapist stretches the patient's joints and muscles to build flexibility. Gradually, patients begin to move their own muscles. Patients then progress to exercises with weights.

Subjects to Study

Mathematics, biology, chemistry, physics, social science, anatomy

Discover More

Talk to the athletic trainer at your school about this type of work. You may be able to check out this occupation by becoming a student trainer in your school athletic department.

Related Jobs

Occupational therapists, corrective therapists, recreational therapists, manual arts therapists, speech pathologists, audiologists, orthotists, prosthetists, respiratory therapists, chiropractors, acupuncturists, athletic trainers

Earnings	Education and Training	Job Outlook
Average	Bachelor's	Increasing rapidly

Physician Assistants

Job Description

Physician assistants always work under the supervision of a physician. They should not be confused with medical assistants (see elsewhere in this book). They do many routine but time-consuming tasks that physicians usually do, such as taking medical records, examining patients, and ordering X rays and tests. They also treat minor injuries.

Something Extra

A physician assistant (PA) is the primary health care provider in many small communities where physicians may be in limited supply. The PA aids patients each day by working in a community clinic while a physician supervises the clinic one or two days each week. The physician can be reached by telephone if the PA needs the physician's advice.

Working Conditions

Physician assistants work in comfortable, well-lighted surroundings. They may work weekends, evenings, or early mornings, depending on the schedule of the supervising physician. Those in surgery may stand for long periods and others do a lot of walking.

Subjects to Study

English, biology, chemistry, mathematics, psychology, social sciences, anatomy, nutrition

Discover More

To learn more about this occupation, send for a free brochure: *Physicians Assistants, Partners in Medicine,* available from the American Academy of Physician Assistants, 950 North Washington St., Alexandria, VA 22314.

Related Jobs

Nurse practitioners, physical therapists, occupational therapists, clinical psychologists, speech and hearing clinicians

Earnings	Education and Training	Job Outlook

High	Bachelor's	Increasing rapidly

Recreational Therapists

Job Description

Recreational therapists use leisure activities to aid and improve the general health and well-being of people with medical problems. They develop these activities based on patients' medical records, medical staff, family, and patients themselves. Activities include sports, arts and crafts, dance, music, group games, and field trips.

Working Conditions

Recreational therapists work in offices and special activity rooms. Most work in hospitals and nursing homes. A 40-hour work week is normal, including some weekends, evenings, and holidays. Physical activity is required because they carry equipment and participate in activities.

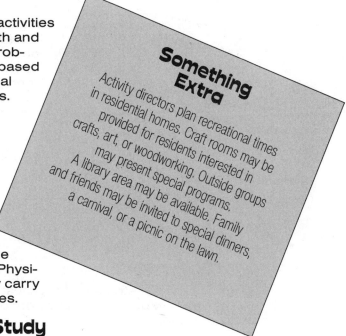

Something Extra

Activity directors plan recreational times in residential homes. Craft rooms may be provided for residents interested in crafts, art, or woodworking. Outside groups may present special programs. A library area may be available. Family and friends may be invited to special dinners, a carnival, or a picnic on the lawn.

Subjects to Study

English, mathematics, speech, communication skills, anatomy, psychology

Discover More

Recreational therapists must feel comfortable around people with disabilities. Get to know someone with a disability—a classmate, an elderly neighbor, or a child. Honestly judge your reaction to this individual.

Related Jobs

Orientation therapists for the blind, art therapists, drama therapists, dance therapists, music therapists, occupational therapists, rehabilitation therapists

Earnings	Education and Training	Job Outlook
Average	Associate/Bachelor's	Increasing

Registered Nurses

Something Extra

In the past, many nurses graduated from diploma programs, offered by hospitals and lasting two or three years. However, fewer nurses are graduating from these programs in recent years. Many choose to attend colleges and universities that offer bachelor's of science degrees in nursing (B.S.N.) because job opportunities are much greater for those with a B.S.N.

Job Description

Registered nurses care for the sick and injured and help people stay well. They observe and record a patient's symptoms and progress, assist physicians, and give out medication. They also develop and manage care plans and instruct patients in proper care. Work settings, such as hospitals, nursing homes, and schools, determine nurses' day-to-day duties.

Working Conditions

Nurses work in medical facilities, homes, and schools. Night, weekend, and holiday work is often required. Nurses must be able to cope with suffering, emergencies, and other stresses. They must guard against hazards such as disease exposure, shocks from electrical equipment, and injury from moving patients.

Subjects to Study

English, mathematics, biology, chemistry, physics, anatomy, psychology, nutrition, health

Discover More

Check out the volunteer program at a hospital in your community. Talk to a nurse who works for your family physician or school. Find out which type of degree he or she has.

Related Jobs

Occupational therapists, paramedics, physical therapists, physician assistants, respiratory therapists

Earnings	Education and Training	Job Outlook
Average	 Professional degree/Bachelor's	 Increasing rapidly

Respiratory Therapists

Job Description

Respiratory therapists care for patients with breathing disorders, from tiny premature babies with underdeveloped lungs to senior citizens with diseased lungs. They perform tests on patients to see if lung problems exist. They connect patients to machines that aid in breathing and teach patients how to use these machines in their homes. Respiratory therapists may also assist in surgery by removing mucus from a patient's lungs so he or she can breathe more easily.

Something Extra

People can live without water for several days and without food for several weeks. But without air, people suffer brain damage after only a few minutes. They die if deprived of air for nine minutes or more. Respiratory therapists provide emergency care for people who stop breathing and need air, such as drowning, heart attack, or stroke victims.

Working Conditions

Respiratory therapists work a 40-hour week, including weekends, evenings, or nights. Most work in hospitals. They stand and walk a lot and may work under the stress of an emergency situation. They must be careful with the gases they use and protect themselves from infectious diseases.

Subjects to Study

Mathematics, health, biology, chemistry, physics

Discover More

Contact the local American Lung Association chapter for information about lung diseases. Talk to someone who has asthma and find out what type of care is used for people with asthma.

Related Jobs

Dialysis technicians, registered nurses, occupational therapists, physical therapists, radiation therapy technologists

Earnings	Education and Training	Job Outlook

Average	Associate	Increasing rapidly

Speech-Language Pathologists and Audiologists

Job Description

Speech-language pathologists work with people who cannot speak or who cannot speak clearly. They teach patients how to make sounds and increase their language skills. They may teach sign language to nonspeaking patients. Audiologists work with people who cannot hear. They recommend treatments such as wearing hearing aids, cleaning the ear canal, or learning lip reading.

Something Extra

Heather Whitestone, Miss America of 1995, is deaf. She communicates through speaking and dancing, and her accomplishments are numerous. She lives very successfully in a hearing world. Helen Keller is another example of a famous deaf person. She communicated to the hearing world as a speaker and writer, expressing her opinions on world issues. Disabilities do not mean defeat.

Working Conditions

Speech-language pathologists and audiologists work at a desk or table. They work about 40 hours each week. These workers must pay close attention to detail and concentrate heavily on their patients. This work is frustrating when a patient is not improving, and dealing with clients and their families can be demanding.

Subjects to Study

English, mathematics, speech, biology, chemistry, physics, psychology

Discover More

Talk to a speech-language pathologist or audiologist in your school and ask how patients are tested. Find out what colleges or universities in your area offer these degrees.

Related Jobs

Occupational therapists, physical therapists, recreational therapists, rehabilitation counselors

Earnings	Education and Training	Job Outlook

High	Master's	Increasing rapidly

Public Relations Specialists

Job Description

Public relations specialists work to maintain a good relationship between their client and the public. They may work for businesses, governments, hospitals, and other organizations. They make the public aware of their client's complishments, often through the media. Writing press releases, preparing speeches, and presenting programs are important duties of this job.

Working Conditions

Public relations specialists work 35 to 40 hours a week, but unpaid overtime is common. Their schedules are often rearranged to meet deadlines, deliver speeches, or travel. In an emergency, they may be on call around the clock.

Something Extra

Whoever holds the job of press secretary for the president of the United States becomes the link between the White House and the world. Information about government activities is distributed through the press secretary. This person schedules news conferences and issues official statements from the president. A major part of the press secretary's job is to keep the president's image in a favorable light.

Subjects to Study

English, creative writing, journalism, psychology, sociology, computer skills, public speaking

Discover More

Look at the business section of a newspaper. Find articles that you think might have come from press releases written by public relations specialists who represent companies.

Related Jobs

Fundraisers, lobbyists, promotion managers, advertising managers, police officers involved in community relations

Earnings	Education and Training	Job Outlook

Average	Bachelor's	Little change

Radio and Television Announcers and Newscasters

Job Description

Announcers and newscasters are usually well-known to radio and television audiences. Radio announcers—or disk jockeys—plan and perform radio programs. They may select and play music, interview guests, and write program material. Television announcers and newscasters prepare and present the news, weather, and sports, although most specialize in one of these areas. These workers are called news anchors, weathercasters, and sports-casters.

Working Conditions

Radio and television announcers and newscasters work in air-conditioned, soundproof studios. They work unusual hours, including very early in the morning or very late at night. Their personal lives are often disrupted by the unusual job demands, but most feel that the advantages, such as creative work and fame, outweigh the disadvantages.

Subjects to Study

English, public speaking, drama, foreign languages, electronics

Discover More

Think of a disk jockey or newscaster whom you like to listen to on the radio or watch on TV. Many of these local stars accept invitations to speak at schools or clubs. Ask your teacher or club leader about arranging for one to speak to your class or group.

Related Jobs

Interpreters, sales workers, public relations specialists, teachers, actors

Earnings	Education and Training	Job Outlook

Very low-average	Specialized training/Bachelor's	Little change

Reporters and Correspondents

Job Description

Reporters and correspondents gather information and write articles that tell the public about events around the world. The articles often present viewpoints on current issues and report the actions of those in power. These workers must investigate leads and interview people. Some take photographs or shoot videos. Radio and television reporters often report "live" from the scene.

Working Conditions

The work of reporters and correspondents is usually hectic, and they are under great stress to meet deadlines. Some work in comfortable, private offices while others work in large rooms filled with noise. Reporting on wars, fires, and floods can be dangerous. This job may demand long hours, irregular schedules, and travel.

Something Extra

"Yellow journalism" is a term used to describe writing about sensational events in an attempt to sell more newspapers. For example, a newspaper might focus on a famous murder trial and the events surrounding it. The term yellow journalism was derived from the yellow ink used in colored comics introduced during the late 1800s.

Subjects to Study

English, journalism, social studies, history, economics, business, speech, computer science, foreign languages

Discover More

Join your school newspaper staff. Try various positions to find out what you like and dislike about the world of journalism.

Related Jobs

Technical writers, advertising copy writers, public relations workers, educational writers, fiction writers, biographers, screen writers, editors

Earnings	Education and Training	Job Outlook

Average	Bachelor's	Little change

Writers and Editors

Job Description

Writers produce books, articles, movies, advertisements, and other written works by gathering information from various sources. They organize their written works, often revising and rewriting, to best express their thoughts. Editors select material for publication, assign stories to writers, and supervise publishing staffs. They frequently write, and always review, rewrite, and correct the work of writers.

Working Conditions

Writers and editors may work in private offices or noisy rooms filled with other writers, telephones, and computers. They usually work 35 to 40 hours a week. Searching for information involves travel, telephone calls, and library research. Overtime and stress when meeting deadlines are common.

Subjects to Study

English, creative writing, journalism, computer skills

Discover More

If your school has a literary magazine, submit some of your written work. Check out the *Writer's Market* for magazines that encourage young writers. Enter a writing contest.

Related Jobs

Newspaper reporters and correspondents, radio and television announcers, advertising and public relations workers, teachers

Earnings	Education and Training	Job Outlook

Low-average	Bachelor's	Little change

Designers

Job Description

Designers create articles, products, and materials that serve a purpose and are also attractive. When making a design, they first determine the needs of the user. Other issues designers consider include materials used, fashion trends, safety, and cost. Designers usually specialize in one area of design, such as appliances, furniture, homes, automobiles, clothing, or flowers.

Working Conditions

Because of their different types of work, designers work varying hours in different places of employment. Their hours may be adjusted to meet their clients' needs, meeting with them on weekends or evenings if needed. Designing can be frustrating when designs are rejected or creativity is limited.

Something Extra

Designers often use a prototype, which is a model of a product. For example, automobile designers may build a fiberglass model of the car they have designed. Like a giant model kit, it is put together to test the design both for eye appeal and for practicality. Mistakes then can be seen and corrected before production starts.

Subjects to Study

Mathematics, drawing, drafting, business, communication skills, English, computer skills

Discover More

Learn about design by helping with the set for a school program. Help select furnishing and accessories for your room. Study an appliance and figure out what could be changed to make it look or work better.

Related Jobs

Visual artists, architects, landscape architects, engineers, photographers, merchandise displayers

Earnings	Education and Training	Job Outlook
Average	Associate/Bachelor's	Little change

Photographers and Camera Operators

Job Description

Photographers and camera operators show people, places, and events clearly or artistically. They use cameras, movie cameras, and camcorders. Most photographers specialize in commercial, portrait, or journalistic photography. Camera operators record documentaries, motion pictures, and industrial films.

Working Conditions

Photographers may work in studios, at local functions, or in dangerous situations such as war zones or disaster areas. Some work regular hours, while others work long, irregular hours and must be available at a moment's notice. They may work in a cramped darkroom and stand with heavy equipment for long periods of time.

Something Extra

Photojournalism shows news events through the lens of the camera. Many photographs have become symbols of historic events. Being in the right place at right time has made some photographers famous. For a photographer, the camera becomes a constant companion to be used at the right moment.

Subjects to Study

English, journalism, mathematics, physics, chemistry, business, accounting

Discover More

Use a camera to record a special event in your life. Try using different types of film. For example, use a roll of black and white film instead of color film to experiment.

Related Jobs

Illustrators, designers, painters, sculptors, editors

Earnings	Education and Training	Job Outlook

Low	Specialized training/Bachelor's	Little change

Visual Artists

Job Description

Visual artists use a variety of methods and materials to communicate ideas, thoughts, and feelings through art. Oils, watercolors, pencils, clay, or other materials are used to create works or images. Visual artists are usually called graphic artists or fine artists. Graphic artists use art to meet the needs of their commercial clients, such as businesses, stores, and publishing firms. Fine artists create works for their own satisfaction and may display their work in museums or galleries.

Something Extra

When she reached her late seventies, Grandma Moses was no longer able to do the farm work she had done all her life. She chose a new occupation—artist. This famous American artist painted scenes of life on the farm. Her style, which resembles the way a child might paint, is known as primitivism.

Working Conditions

Graphic and fine artists work in studios located in office buildings or in their homes. Odors from glues, paint, and other materials may be present. Graphic artists employed by publishing companies and studios work standard 40-hour weeks. Self-employed graphic artists must sell their services to clients, which requires much effort and time.

Subjects to Study

English, communication skills, speech, art, anatomy, business, computer science, mathematics

Discover More

Visit an art museum or art fair. Look at the different types of artworks and try to figure out which materials were used to create them.

Related Jobs

Account executives or creative directors, architects, display workers, floral designers, industrial designers, interior designers, landscape architects, photographers, art and design teachers

Earnings	Education and Training	Job Outlook

Low	Specialized training/ Bachelor's	Little change

Actors, Directors, and Producers

Something Extra

Very few actors ever become stars. Most actors struggle to become accepted in their profession. Some work as "extras," actors who have no speaking parts. Others teach drama classes offered to the public. Actors often work at other jobs to earn a living, such as bartending or waiting tables, when they are between acting roles.

Job Description

Actors, directors, and producers make words come alive for their audiences. Actors create their roles using body and facial expressions, costumes, and words. Directors interpret plays and scripts, audition actors, and conduct rehearsals. Producers select productions, arrange the financing, and decide the size of the production and the budget.

Working Conditions

Actors work long hours and often travel. They experience unsure employment and rejections. Most work under hot lights or in heavy costumes. All are required to memorize lines quickly and rehearse until the director is satisfied. Directors and producers work under stress to meet schedules, stay within budgets, and resolve any problems.

Subjects to Study

English, public speaking, drama, music, dance

Discover More

Participate in a school or community theatrical production.

Related Jobs

Dancers, choreographers, disk jockeys, drama teachers or coaches, radio and television announcers, playwrights, scriptwriters, stage managers, costume designers, makeup artists, hair stylists, lighting designers, set designers

Earnings	Education and Training	Job Outlook

Very low-very high	Specialized training/ Bachelor's	Increasing rapidly

Dancers and Choreographers

Job Description

Dancers express ideas and stories through the movement of their bodies. Dance styles include classical ballet, modern dance, and folk dance. Dancers perform in musicals, operas, television, movies, videos, and commercials. Choreographers create dances and instruct dancers.

Working Conditions

Dancers work strenuously. They rehearse long hours every day, including weekends and holidays. Dancers often work late hours because many performances are in the evening. Due to physical demands, most dancers retire by their late thirties. Some continue to work in dance as teachers, choreographers, and artistic directors.

Something Extra

Serious ballet training traditionally begins at the age of 10, although early training can start as young as 3 years old. Most dancers have their professional auditions by the age of 17 or 18. The training and practice for professional ballet dancers never ends. They have daily lessons for an hour or more and additional practices and rehearsals.

Subjects to Study

Music, dance, physical education, drama, English, history, literature

Discover More

Attend a ballet performance, a dance company presentation, or any performance involving dancers. Talk to someone who takes dance lessons. Ask about practice schedules and the need for physical fitness.

Related Jobs

Ice skaters, dance critics, dance instructors, dance notators, dance therapists, athletes

Earnings	Education and Training	Job Outlook

Average	Specialized training	Little change

Musicians

Something Extra

Computers are often used these days in composing music. A musical keyboard is linked to a computer that compiles the digital information into musical notes while the musician plays. The composition can be programmed into the computer, which can play back the musical piece.

Job Description

Musicians play instruments, sing, write music, or conduct groups in instrumental or vocal performances. They may perform in groups or alone, in front of live audiences, on radio, or in recording studios. They must spend a lot of time practicing and rehearsing for performances.

Working Conditions

Musicians work at night and on the weekends and travel to perform. They spend a lot of time practicing and rehearsing. Because many musicians find only part-time work or experience unemployment, they may take full-time jobs in other occupations to support themselves. Many work in cities where entertainment and recording activities are concentrated, such as New York, Los Angeles, and Nashville.

Subjects to Study

Vocal music, instrumental music, English, mathematics, business

Discover More

Participate in your school band, jazz band, choral group, or swing choir.

Related Jobs

Booking agents, concert managers, music publishers, music store owners and managers, salespersons of records, sheet music, and musical instruments

Earnings	Education and Training	Job Outlook

Very low-very high	Specialized training/Bachelor's	Little change

Technicians and Related Support Occupations

Cardiovascular Technologists and Technicians

Something Extra

An electrocardiogram (EKG) is a test commonly given before an operation or as part of a physical examination. Cardiovascular technicians and technologists administer an EKG by attaching electrodes to a patient's arms, chest, and legs. A machine records the heart's electrical impulses. A treadmill test may be done in which the patient walks on a treadmill while the test is performed.

Job Description

Cardiovascular technologists and technicians help doctors treat heart and blood vessel diseases. They use a variety of tests, monitor the results, and prepare patients for tests. They may schedule patient appointments, type doctors' reports, keep patient files, and care for the testing equipment.

Working Conditions

Technologists and technicians work a 40-hour week, including Saturdays and Sundays. They may be on call at night or on weekends. This job can be stressful because workers are in contact with patients who have serious heart problems.

Subjects to Study

English, communication skills, mathematics, computer skills, health

Discover More

Talk to an EKG supervisor or a cardiologist at a hospital. Ask a technician about on-the-job training. The hospital staff can supply information about this occupation.

Related Jobs

Radiologic technologists, diagnostic medical sonographers, electroencephalographic technologists, perfusionists, respiratory therapists

Earnings	Education and Training	Job Outlook

Low	Specialized training/Associate	Increasing

Clinical Laboratory Technologists and Technicians

Job Description

Clinical laboratory technologists and technicians perform medical tests to help detect, diagnose, and treat diseases. They match blood types, analyze body fluids, test for drug levels in blood, and look for abnormal cells. They analyze the test results and relay them to doctors. Automated equipment allows these workers to do more than one test at a time.

Working Conditions

Clinical laboratory technologists and technicians work in clean, well-lighted labs. They may work in shifts, at night, and on weekends and are on their feet much of the time. They must protect themselves from infectious specimens.

Something Extra

When a patient complains of a sore throat, a doctor may order a test called a throat culture. In a throat culture, a small amount of fluid from the throat is placed on microscopic slides. These slides are sent to the laboratory to be checked for streptococcus bacteria, which causes infection in humans. The doctor analyzes the results of the test to treat the patient.

Subjects to Study

English, biology, chemistry, physics, computer skills, mathematics

Discover More

Think about medical tests that you or someone in your family has had. Who took the tests? Where were the tests taken? How long did it take to get the test results? Who gave the test results to you?

Related Jobs

Water purification and other chemists, science technicians, crime laboratory analysts, food testers, veterinary laboratory technicians

Earnings	Education and Training	Job Outlook
Low-average	Associate/Bachelor's	Little change

Dental Hygienists

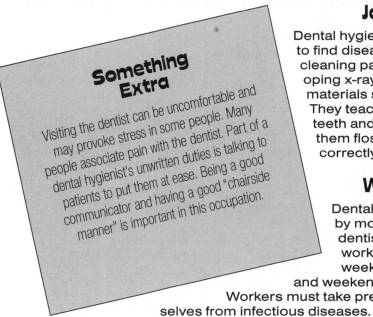

Something Extra

Visiting the dentist can be uncomfortable and may provoke stress in some people. Many people associate pain with the dentist. Part of a dental hygienist's unwritten duties is talking to patients to put them at ease. Being a good communicator and having a good "chairside manner" is important in this occupation.

Job Description

Dental hygienists examine teeth and gums to find disease. They assist dentists by cleaning patients' teeth, taking and developing x-rays, and applying protective materials such as fluoride to the teeth. They teach patients how to clean their teeth and prevent cavities by helping them floss and select toothbrushes correctly.

Working Conditions

Dental hygienists may be employed by more than one dentist because dentists often hire hygienists to work only two or three days a week. Full-time, part-time, evening, and weekend work is widely available. Workers must take precautions to protect themselves from infectious diseases.

Subjects to Study

English, speech, biology, chemistry, mathematics, nutrition, anatomy

Discover More

On your next visit to the dentist, talk to the hygienist who checks your teeth. Find out why the hygienist chose this occupation. Ask about the hours he or she works and the training needed for this job.

Related Jobs

Dental assistants, ophthalmic medical assistants, podiatric assistants, office nurses, medical assistants, physician assistants

Earnings	Education and Training	Job Outlook

Low-average	Associate	Increasing

Dispensing Opticians

Job Description

Dispensing opticians fit glasses and contact lenses using prescriptions written by eye doctors. They help customers find the frames that fit their needs, write out the orders, and fit the glasses when they are completed. Keeping customer records and tracking inventory and sales are also duties of this occupation.

Working Conditions

Dispensing opticians work in small and large stores where they deal directly with customers. These workers must take precautions against glass cutting, chemicals, and machinery when preparing lenses. They work 40 hours each week, and some work evenings, weekends, or part-time.

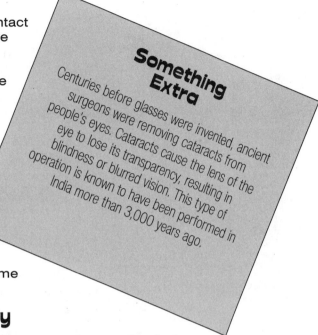

Something Extra

Centuries before glasses were invented, ancient surgeons were removing cataracts from people's eyes. Cataracts cause the lens of the eye to lose its transparency, resulting in blindness or blurred vision. This type of operation is known to have been performed in India more than 3,000 years ago.

Subjects to Study

English, speech, physics, anatomy, algebra, geometry, mechanical drawing

Discover More

Visit an optical store in your community. Observe the wide selection of eyewear and decide which frames best fit your face. Talk to one of the dispensing opticians about this type of work.

Related Jobs

Jewelers, artificial eye makers, ophthalmic laboratory technicians, dental laboratory technicians, prosthetics technicians, camera repairers, watch repairers

Earnings	Education and Training	Job Outlook
Low	Specialized training/Associate	Increasing

EEG Technologists

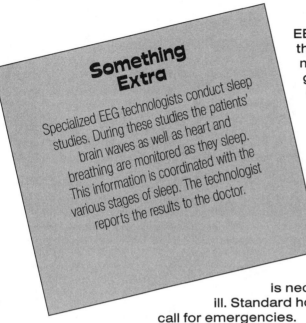

Something Extra

Specialized EEG technologists conduct sleep studies. During these studies the patients' brain waves as well as heart and breathing are monitored as they sleep. This information is coordinated with the various stages of sleep. The technologist reports the results to the doctor.

Job Description

EEG technologists record brain waves through tests performed by a special machine called an electroencephalograph machine. These tests are used by doctors who study the brain to find brain tumors, help stroke victims, and make other medical decisions. They are also used to determine brain activity in patients in comas.

Working Conditions

EEG technologists work in clean, well-lighted surroundings and spend about half of their time on their feet. Lifting and helping patients is necessary because many patients are very ill. Standard hours are normal, although some are on call for emergencies.

Subjects to Study

Health, biology, mathematics, English

Discover More

Your brain is like a computer. Learn more about it by checking your library for books and videos about the "control room" of your body. Find out if you are a left-brained or right-brained person.

Related Jobs

Radiologic technologists, nuclear medicine technologists, perfusionists, EKG technologists

Earnings	Education and Training	Job Outlook

Low	Specialized training/Associate	Increasing rapidly

Emergency Medical Technicians

Job Description

Emergency medical technicians (EMTs) drive specially equipped vehicles, often called ambulances, to the scenes of emergencies. They determine the medical condition of patients at the scene and give emergency care following strict guidelines for which procedures they may perform. They take the patients to a hospital for further medical help and report their observations about patient condition to the hospital staff.

Something Extra

In times of disaster and war, emergency medical care becomes very important. During the Civil War in the United States, Clara Barton organized nursing care for the Union soldiers. Later in the 1880s, she founded the American Red Cross, which is still a major form of aid to victims of emergencies and disasters.

Working Conditions

EMTs work indoors and outdoors in all kinds of weather. Hours are irregular and days are often long. The work is physically strenuous and stressful. Some patients are violent due to drug overdoses, and EMTs may be exposed to diseases. These workers are employed by fire departments, hospitals, and private ambulance services.

Subjects to Study

Driver education, health, biology, chemistry, anatomy, English, foreign languages

Discover More

Check with the Red Cross in your area to register for a first aid or CPR course. You can learn how to save another person's life and be helpful in different types of emergencies.

Related Jobs

Police officers, firefighters, air traffic controllers, workers in health occupations, members of the Air Force

Earnings	Education and Training	Job Outlook
Low	Specialized training	Increasing

Licensed Practical Nurses

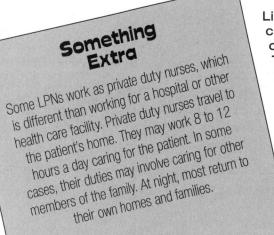

Something Extra

Some LPNs work as private duty nurses, which is different than working for a hospital or other health care facility. Private duty nurses travel to the patient's home. They may work 8 to 12 hours a day caring for the patient. In some cases, their duties may involve caring for other members of the family. At night, most return to their own homes and families.

Job Description

Licensed practical nurses (LPNs) provide care for the sick and injured under the direction of doctors or registered nurses. They provide basic bedside care, helping patients with bathing, dressing, and personal hygiene, feeding them, and caring for their emotional needs. They are responsible for keeping patients as comfortable as possible. Some LPNs help deliver, care for, and feed infants.

Working Conditions

Licensed practical nurses work a 40-hour week, including nights, weekends, and holidays. This job is physically tiring and stressful. LPNs must protect themselves from exposure to infectious diseases. Most work in hospitals, nursing homes, and private homes.

Subjects to Study

English, health, anatomy, psychology, first aid, nutrition, home economics courses

Discover More

Licensed practical nursing programs are offered in some high school vocational programs. Talk to a counselor about this type of program and find out if any are available through high schools in your area.

Related Jobs

Emergency medical technicians, social service aides, human service workers, teacher aides

Earnings	Education and Training	Job Outlook

Low	Specialized training	Increasing

Medical Record Technicians

Job Description

Medical record technicians organize patients' medical information. They first make sure that all necessary forms have been signed and that the information is on a computer file. Much of the information, such as treatment plans or diagnoses, is assigned a code by the technician. Sometimes, they enlist the help of doctors if they have questions about a record.

Working Conditions

Medical record technicians work a 40-hour week with some overtime. They may work day, evening, or night shifts. Their work requires accuracy, so they must pay close attention to detail. Because much of their work is done on a computer, they may be prone to eyestrain and muscle pain.

Something Extra

Unlike most health care workers, medical records technicians have little contact with patients. However, their work greatly affects patients. The information they record is used to determine health insurance payments, improve patient care, and supply doctors with the patient's medical history.

Subjects to Study

English, computer skills, anatomy, biology

Discover More

Learn more about medical record technicians and an independent study program which is available by writing to: American Health Information Management Association, 919 N. Michigan Ave., Suite 1400, Chicago, IL 60611.

Related Jobs

Medical secretaries, medical transcribers, medical writers, medical illustrators

Earnings	Education and Training	Job Outlook
Low	Associate	Increasing rapidly

Nuclear Medicine Technologists

Job Description

Nuclear medicine technologists give radioactive drugs to patients, which are used to diagnose and treat disease. Using a camera, they follow the drug as it enters the patient's body and record the effects the drug has on the patient's body. They keep patients' records, including the amount of drug given and the amount disposed of.

Something Extra

In 1898, Marie Curie, a French chemist, and her husband Pierre discovered the element radium. She was the first major woman scientist of modern times. Marie Curie was the only person ever to receive the Nobel Prize in two different sciences—chemistry and physics.

Working Conditions

Nuclear medicine technologists use protective devices to keep radiation exposure to a minimum and wear badges that measure radiation levels. They work a 40-hour week, which may include evening or weekend hours, and are often on call. Physical strength is required because they often lift and move patients.

Subjects to Study

Physical sciences, chemistry, physics, mathematics, computer science

Discover More

To learn more about radiation medicine, check the library for books about individuals who have battled cancer. Books have been written by children, teenagers, and adults who have undergone radiation treatment to fight cancer and other diseases.

Related Jobs

Radiologic technologists, diagnostic medical sonographers, cardiology technologists, electroencephalographic (EEG) technologists, clinical laboratory technologists, perfusionists, respiratory therapists

Earnings	Education and Training	Job Outlook

Average	Associate/Bachelor's	Increasing rapidly

Radiologic Technologists

Job Description

Radiologic technologists produce x-rays and other diagnostic images that show a picture of the inside of a patient's body. Some technologists also use radiation to treat cancer patients. The affected part of the patient's body receives treatment while other body parts are protected from the radiation. These workers must follow doctors' instructions to ensure that they, the patients, and coworkers are protected from overexposure.

Something Extra

Using the technique of ultrasound, which is composed of high frequency sound waves, a sonographer takes a picture of a baby before it is born. The image of the baby is projected on a screen for the mother to see. A printout of the screen image can be used by the doctor to detect any abnormalities.

Working Conditions

Radiologic technologists work about 40 hours each week and may have evening, weekend, or on call hours. They use radiation protective devices and wear radiation measuring badges. Some work from specially equipped vans. Most work is done at radiologic machines, but some is performed at patients' bedsides. Because they work with extremely ill and dying patients, they may experience emotional burn-out.

Subjects to Study

Mathematics, physics, chemistry, biology, English

Discover More

Ask your mother if she had an ultrasound taken before you were born. Find out what was done to get your "before birth" picture.

Related Jobs

Nuclear medicine technologists, cardiovascular technologists and technicians, perfusionists, respiratory therapists, clinical laboratory technologists, electroencephalographic (EEG) technologists

Earnings	Education and Training	Job Outlook
Low-average	Associate/Bachelor's	Increasing rapidly

Surgical Technologists

Job Description

Surgical technologists set up equipment in the operating room, prepare patients for surgery, and take patients to and from the operating room. They help the surgical team "scrub" and put on gloves, masks, and surgical clothing. During an operation, they assist with supplies and instruments and operate lights and equipment. Following the operation, they restock the operating room.

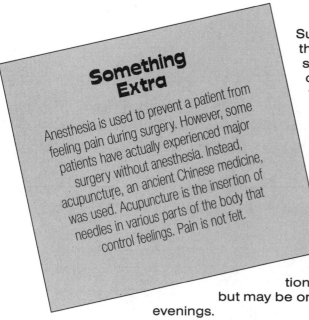

Something Extra

Anesthesia is used to prevent a patient from feeling pain during surgery. However, some patients have actually experienced major surgery without anesthesia. Instead, acupuncture, an ancient Chinese medicine, was used. Acupuncture is the insertion of needles in various parts of the body that control feelings. Pain is not felt.

Working Conditions

Surgical technologists work in clean, cool, well-lighted environments. They stand for long periods of time and must be alert during operations. They work a regular 40-hour week, but may be on call for emergencies on weekends and evenings.

Subjects to Study

Health, biology, chemistry, mathematics, anatomy, English

Discover More

Talk to someone in your family who has had an operation. Find out what they remember about the procedure. What type of anesthesia was used?

Related Jobs

Licensed practical nurses, respiratory therapy technicians, medical laboratory assistants, medical assistants, dental assistants, optometric assistants, physical therapy aides

Earnings	Education and Training	Job Outlook
Low	Specialized training/Associate	Increasing rapidly

Aircraft Pilots

Job Description

Aircraft pilots fly airplanes and helicopters, performing tasks such as delivering passengers and cargo, testing aircraft, dusting crops, and fighting forest fires. Pilots may work for large airlines, charter services, or businesses. They must plan flights, check the aircraft and weather conditions, and keep records of each flight.

Working Conditions

By law, pilots cannot fly more than 100 hours each month. Excellent health, hearing, and eyesight are required. Pilots' work involves being away from home and irregular hours. Being responsible for the safety of passengers and crew can be mentally stressful. Test pilots, crop dusters, and police helicopter pilots may be exposed to physical dangers.

Something Extra

When an air crash occurs, investigators search for the "black box" at the crash site. The black box is the flight recorder. Although it is a sensitive recording device, it is rugged enough to survive a crash. It records vital information about the aircraft's performance. The black box helps investigators learn what happened and why the crash occurred. This information can be used to help prevent other air crashes.

Subjects to Study

English, mathematics, computer skills, electronics, physical science, physical education, foreign languages

Discover More

To learn more about flying and various aircraft, visit an airport, a military base, or an air museum. If you get an opportunity to take a flight, you may be allowed to visit the cockpit if you make arrangements with the flight crew.

Related Jobs

Air traffic controllers, air traffic dispatchers

Earnings	Education and Training	Job Outlook

Very high	Associate/Bachelor's/Specialized training	Increasing

Air Traffic Controllers

Job Description

Air traffic controllers are responsible for the safe and efficient movement of airport traffic both in the air and on the ground. Using radar and visual observation, they direct landings, take-offs, and ground movement of aircraft. They keep aircraft safe distances apart during flights and inform pilots of current weather conditions. In emergencies they may search for missing aircraft.

Working Conditions

Air traffic controllers work 40-hour weeks with possible overtime hours. They may work nights, weekends, and holidays. This work requires total concentration to keep track of several aircraft at one time and give pilots correct information. Working rapidly and efficiently during busy times is important. Having responsibility for the safety of the crew and passengers of several aircraft can be stressful.

Something Extra

Before the pilot radios the terminal to request a landing, a controller has already observed the plane on a radar screen. The controller may direct the pilot to a runway if it is clear for landing, or the plane may be put in a traffic pattern away from other planes until landing is possible. When the plane is ready to land, another controller guides the plane the last mile to the runway. To avoid accidents, departing planes are instructed to wait. A ground controller directs the landed plane along the taxiways to the gate, where passengers will leave the plane.

Subjects to Study

English, mathematics, computer skills, physics, physical science, foreign languages, electronics

Discover More

Observe air traffic controllers at work in the air terminal or on the ground at an airport. Obtain a copy of the *Air Traffic Controller Announcement*, an informative pamphlet about this occupation. Call the U.S. Job Information Center in your area. Look under U.S. Government, Office of Personal Management, in the *Yellow Pages*. If no number is listed, dial the toll-free number 1-800-555-1212 and ask for the number of the Office of Personal Management Job Information Center in your area.

Related Jobs

Airline-radio operators, air traffic dispatchers

Earnings	Education and Training	Job Outlook

Very high	Bachelor's/ Specialized training	Little change

Broadcast Technicians

Job Description

Broadcast technicians work with electronic equipment used to record and transmit radio and television programs. They operate, install, and repair equipment such as microphones, television cameras, tape recorders, and antennas. They may give technical directions to studio personnel during a broadcast. Movie soundtracks are developed by broadcast technicians.

Working Conditions

Broadcast technicians work 40-hour weeks. Holiday, weekend, and night work is usual. Most work indoors. Disasters or crime news stories may require working under unpleasant conditions. Setting up equipment may require heavy lifting or climbing. Movie work may be done on a tight schedule.

Something Extra

Sound mixers are technicians in the movie industry. Using a process called dubbing, mixers produce the sound track for a movie. Sitting at a console facing the movie screen, the technician is responsible for certain sounds, which are faded in or out according to a script. The volume of the sound is also controlled. All the sounds are blended on a master sound track, which is used when the movie is shown.

Subjects to Study

Mathematics, physics, electronics, English, computer skills

Discover More

Build your own electronic equipment using a hobby kit. Check a toy or hobby store to see what type of equipment is available. Operating a "ham" or amateur radio station is great experience for this occupation.

Related Jobs

Drafters, engineering and science technicians, surveyors, air traffic controllers, radiologic technologists, respiratory therapy workers, cardiovascular technologists and technicians, EEG technicians, medical laboratory technicians

Earnings	Education and Training	Job Outlook

Low-very high	Associate/Bachelor's	Little change

Computer Programmers

Something Extra

Applications programmers write software that does a specific job, such as keeping the inventory records for a business or guiding a missile after it has been fired. Systems programmers maintain software that controls an entire computer system. Because they understand the entire computer system, they may help applications programmers in software development.

Job Description

Computer programmers write, update, and maintain software that allows computers to work. Programmers provide detailed, step-by-step instructions for the computer. When a program is written, they test it. If the software does not produce the desired information, the programmer must correct the errors until the program works effectively.

Working Conditions

Computer programmers work in comfortable offices. They usually work 40 hours each week. However, they may work unusual hours in order to be able to use the computer when it is available. If problems or deadlines occur, they may work longer hours. Eyestrain, back ache, and hand and wrist problems are some difficulties that may develop from this job.

Subjects to Study

Computer skills, computer programming, data processing, mathematics, physical science, English, keyboarding

Discover More

Learn to use a computer. If you don't have one in your home, check your local library or school for times that computers are available for use. Join a computer club. Manuals are available to help you learn how to use a variety of computer programs.

Related Jobs

Statisticians, engineers, financial analysts, accountants, auditors, actuaries, and operations research analysts

Earnings	Education and Training	Job Outlook

Average-high	Bachelor's	Increasing

Drafters

Job Description

Drafters prepare drawings used to build everything from spacecraft to bridges. Using rough sketches done by others, they produce detailed technical drawings with specific information to create a finished product. Drafters use technical handbooks, tables, calculators, and computers to do their work. They often specialize in an area such as architecture, electronics, or aeronautics.

Something Extra

Drafters use computer-aided drafting (CAD) systems to create drawings on a video screen. When CAD systems were first introduced, many people thought that a new occupation (CAD operator) would result. But now it is obvious that to use the CAD system, drafting skills are still needed. A drafter needs both the traditional skills of the trade and the ability to use the computer to create technical drawings.

Working Conditions

Drafters work in well-lit offices or rooms. Sitting at drawing boards or computer terminals for long periods of time can cause backaches and eyestrain. Using the computer keyboard for CAD may result in problems such as carpal tunnel syndrome.

Subjects to Study

Mathematics, physical science, drafting, art courses, computer skills, English, industrial arts courses

Discover More

Try creating your own drawing of a structure or some type of machine. You may choose to use paper and pencil or a computer drawing program. Books about drafting are available at the library.

Related Jobs

Architects, landscape architects, engineers, engineering technicians, science technicians, photogrammetrists, cartographers, surveyors

Earnings	Education and Training	Job Outlook
Average	Associate	Little change

Engineering Technicians

Job Description

Engineering technicians use science, engineering, and mathematics to solve problems in research, manufacturing, sales, construction, and customer service. They often assist engineers and scientists with experiments and developing prototypes of new equipment. Some supervise production workers or check the quality of products. Like engineers, they specialize in an area such as mechanics, electronics, or chemicals.

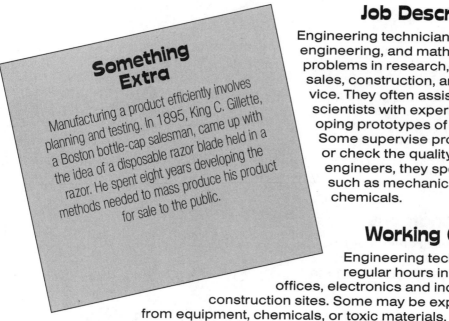

Something Extra

Manufacturing a product efficiently involves planning and testing. In 1895, King C. Gillette, a Boston bottle-cap salesman, came up with the idea of a disposable razor blade held in a razor. He spent eight years developing the methods needed to mass produce his product for sale to the public.

Working Conditions

Engineering technicians work regular hours in laboratories, offices, electronics and industrial plants, or construction sites. Some may be exposed to hazards from equipment, chemicals, or toxic materials.

Subjects to Study

Mathematics, physics, chemistry, electronics, English, industrial arts courses

Discover More

Try a project that requires step-by-step construction. Browse through books and magazines for an idea that interests you. Write out the steps you will follow to complete the project. Then follow them to finish the project.

Related Jobs

Science technicians, drafters, surveyors, broadcast technicians, health technologists and technicians

Earnings	Education and Training	Job Outlook
Low	Associate	Little change

Library Technicians

Job Description

Library technicians assist librarians in ordering, coding, and organizing library materials. They help users find materials and information. Some help maintain audiovisual equipment, prepare displays, and supervise other support staff. Computerized information systems allow technicians to handle more technical and user services than they once did.

Working Conditions

Library technicians work with the public, answering questions. Some spend hours working at desks or computer terminals. Eyestrain and headaches may be caused by this work. Technicians in public and university libraries may work evenings and weekends. Those working in schools and special business libraries work normal hours. Some work, such as calculating statistics, can be boring, while searching for information can be a challenge.

Something Extra

Many American adults are not able to read the words you are reading right now. Libraries have become a source of help for these men and women. Throughout the United States, libraries are teaching other adults to read. Libraries provide training for volunteers, books for teaching, and meeting places for volunteers and learners.

Subjects to Study

English, literature, mathematics, computer skills, sciences, business courses

Discover More

Check with your local library to see if they use volunteers to help with library needs. Youth volunteers may shelve materials and help with other simple library tasks. Many libraries have an organization that supervises volunteers. You may be able to join this organization.

Related Jobs

Library clerks, information clerks, record clerks, medical record technicians, title searchers, museum technicians, teacher aides, legal assistants, engineering and science technicians

Earnings	Education and Training	Job Outlook

Low	High school/Associate/Bachelor's	Little change

Paralegals

Job Description

Paralegals assist lawyers without actually practicing law. They cannot set fees, give legal advice, or present court cases. They do research, investigate facts about cases, write reports used to decide how cases will be handled, and keep files. They may meet with clients to gain information about a case. Some paralegals have a wide variety of tasks, while others specialize in one area.

Working Conditions

Paralegals work in offices and law libraries. Traveling is sometimes necessary. A 40-hour week is normal, but deadlines may cause longer hours. Some work temporarily during busy times. The work can be unchallenging. Experienced paralegals have more varied duties.

Subjects to Study

English, mathematics, business courses, keyboarding, computer skills

Discover More

Contact a law firm or a legal aid society. Ask to talk to a paralegal. Find out what his or her duties involve. Ask how he or she became interested in this occupation and what type of training he or she has.

Related Jobs

Abstractors, claim examiners, compliance and enforcement inspectors, occupational safety and health workers, patent agents, police officers, title examiners

Earnings	Education and Training	Job Outlook

Average	Associate/Bachelor's	Increasing rapidly

Science Technicians

Job Description

Science technicians use science and mathematics to solve research problems, and to investigate, invent, and help improve products. They set up, operate, and maintain laboratory equipment, monitor experiments, and record results. They may specialize in agriculture, biology, chemistry, or other sciences.

Working Conditions

Science technicians normally work regular hours in laboratories. Some irregular hours may be needed to check experiments. Agricultural and petroleum technicians work outdoors. Some technicians may be exposed to chemicals, radiation, or disease-causing organisms.

Something Extra

Developing uses for agricultural crops can be important to areas of the country that grow those crops. George Washington Carver's work is an excellent example of this. Carver, the son of slaves, developed hundreds of uses for two Southern crops: the peanut and the sweet potato. His work aided the South's economy and made him a nationally recognized scientist.

Subjects to Study

Sciences, mathematics, English, computer skills, communication skills

Discover More

Learn about the equipment used in a laboratory. Learn how computers are used in experiments. Visit a laboratory and talk with the technicians about their work.

Related Jobs

Engineering technicians, broadcast technicians, drafters, health technologists and technicians, agriculture and forestry workers

Earnings	Education and Training	Job Outlook

Low-average	Associate/Bachelor's	Little change

Marketing and Sales Occupations

Cashiers

Job Description

Businesses hire cashiers to sell their merchandise. Cashiers add up customers' bills, take their money, and give change. They also fill out charge forms for credit cards and give receipts. Cashiers are responsible for the money they collect during their shift. Cash registers, scanners, and computers are used regularly in this type of work.

Working Conditions

Cashiers work weekends, evenings, and holidays. About half of cashiers work part-time. Because stores are busiest during the holidays, vacation time between Thanksgiving and the first part of January is restricted. Cashiers work indoors and are not allowed to leave their stations without the supervisor's permission because they are responsible for large amounts of money. Dealing with angry customers can be stressful.

Subjects to Study

Mathematics, English, speech, computer skills, typing, business

Discover More

Volunteer to help with a church, club, or family rummage sale as a cashier. Make sure the cash drawer has the needed amount of money to make change for the customers.

Related Jobs

Food counter clerks, bank tellers, counter and rental clerks, sales clerks

Earnings	Education and Training	Job Outlook

Very low	High school	Little change

Counter and Rental Clerks

Job Description

Counter and rental clerks take orders, calculate fees, receive payments, and accept returns. They answer questions about product availability, cost, and rental provisions. They must know about the company's services and policies. Some fill out forms and tickets by hand, but most use computers and scanners.

Working Conditions

Counter and rental clerks often work evenings and weekends. About half work part-time. Working conditions can be pleasant, but standing and being confined to a small area are often a part of this job. Dealing with unsatisfied or angry customers can be stressful.

Something Extra

Rental clerks become a part of students' lives when they prepare for "Prom Night." Tuxedos, gowns, and accessories are often rented from the appropriate business through the help of rental and counter clerks. Transportation in a limousine is also available for a rental fee, as are prom decorations.

Subjects to Study

Mathematics, English, speech, communication skills, writing skills, computer skills

Discover More

At a park or recreation area, rent a bike, paddle boat, or pair of in-line skates. Observe what the rental clerk does to rent the item and ensure that it is returned.

Related Jobs

Cashiers, retail sales workers, food counter clerks, postal service clerks, bank tellers

Earnings	Education and Training	Job Outlook

Very low	High school	Increasing

Insurance Agents and Brokers

Job Description

Insurance agents and brokers sell individuals, families, and businesses insurance policies which protect against loss. Different types of insurance include life, health, automobile, and medical. These workers help customers choose the policy that best meets their needs. Insurance agents work for one insurance company, while brokers are independent and sell insurance for several different companies.

Something Extra

Besides houses, cars, and businesses, people often choose to insure unusual items. Musicians have insured their hands and instruments. Racing horses and performing animals have been insured. Artifacts and artwork may be insured. Just about anything can be insured if the owner is willing to pay the insurance company's fee.

Working Conditions

Most insurance agents and brokers work in small offices. However, most of their time is spent outside of the office meeting with clients. They often arrange their own schedules and evening and weekend appointments are common. Many work more than 40 hours a week.

Subjects to Study

Mathematics, accounting, economics, government, psychology, sociology, speech, computer skills

Discover More

Talk to your parents about the types of insurance they have. Ask them what insurance, if any, is available through their employers. Ask how they chose their insurance plans.

Related Jobs

Real estate agents and brokers, securities and financial services sales representatives, financial advisors, estate planning specialists, manufacturers' sales workers

Earnings	Education and Training	Job Outlook

Average	Bachelor's	Increasing

Manufacturers' and Wholesale Sales Representatives

Job Description

Manufacturers' and wholesale sales representatives sell products to businesses, government agencies, and other institutions. They answer questions about their products and show clients how these products can meet their companies' needs and save money. They also take orders and resolve any problems or complaints about their merchandise.

Working Conditions

Manufacturers' and wholesale sales representatives travel frequently, sometimes for several days or weeks at a time. Most work more than 40 hours a week. Dealing with different people, handling competition, and meeting sales goals make this job demanding. Because their earnings are based on what they sell, they are under a lot of pressure to make sales.

Something Extra

Sales representatives are paid "on commission." This means that they are paid on the amount of sales they make and they do not receive a regular paycheck. Many sales pay off in a large commission check while few or no sales mean little or no money. Salespeople must learn to budget and pay their bills knowing that their income is uncertain.

Subjects to Study

Mathematics, English, speech, communication skills, accounting, business

Discover More

Think of businesses in your community, such as hospitals, grocery stores, and restaurants, that may be clients of manufacturers' sales representatives. What type of products do you think these businesses might buy?

Related Jobs

Retail service agents, real estate agents, insurance agents, securities sales workers, wholesale and retail buyers

Earnings	Education and Training	Job Outlook
Average	High school/Bachelor's	Little change

Real Estate Agents, Brokers, and Appraisers

Something Extra

Looking at many different houses can be confusing to people who want to buy a home. Videotapes now help home buyers remember features of homes they have visited. Some agents also use videos to show homes to clients who are moving from one area to another.

Job Description

Real estate agents, brokers, and appraisers help people buy and sell homes and rental properties. Real estate agents show homes, help get financing, and make sure that the terms of the contract are met. Brokers also rent and manage properties. Appraisers estimate the worth of a property. All must have a thorough knowledge of the housing market in their community.

Working Conditions

Agents, brokers, and appraisers spend much of their time outside their offices working with clients. Many work part-time and have other careers aside from real estate. Most are paid on commission.

Subjects to Study

Mathematics, English, economics, business, computer skills

Discover More

Free real estate and rental magazines are often available in displays at grocery stores or gas stations. Look through these to find out what homes and properties are available in your community. How much do homes and apartments in your area cost?

Related Jobs

Automotive sales workers, securities and financial services sales workers, insurance agents and brokers, yacht brokers, travel agents, manufacturers' representatives, art appraisers

Earnings	Education and Training	Job Outlook

Average-very high	Specialized training/Bachelor's	Increasing

Retail Sales Workers

Job Description

Retail sales workers help customers choose and buy items from sweaters and cosmetics to lumber and plumbing. Their primary job is to interest customers in whatever merchandise they are selling. They also make out sales checks, take payments, bag purchases, and give change and receipts. Most sales workers are held responsible for the money in their cash register.

Working Conditions

Retail sales workers stand for long periods of time and often need a supervisor's permission to leave the sales area. Many work evenings and weekends, with longer working hours during peak shopping times such as Christmas. Vacation time is usually restricted from Thanksgiving until early January. These workers need patience to deal with demanding customers.

Something Extra

Personal shoppers closely assist consumers in buying particular items. In a department store, they may help a customer update his or her wardrobe. Some personal shoppers choose items based only on information provided by the customer. In grocery stores, they buy and arrange for delivery of groceries to people who are unable to leave their homes.

Subjects to Study

Mathematics, English, speech

Discover More

Observe sales workers as you are shopping. What tasks do they perform? How do they try to interest customers in their store's merchandise? How do they help customers?

Related Jobs

Manufacturers' and wholesale trade sales workers, service sales representatives, counter and rental clerks, real estate sales agents, wholesale and retail buyers, insurance sales workers, cashiers

Earnings	Education and Training	Job Outlook

Very low	Specialized training	Little change

Securities and Financial Services Sales Representatives

Something Extra

"On Wall Street today stock prices rose." This statement, or one similar to it, is usually heard on the nightly news. Wall Street is a street in New York City where the New York Stock Exchange and other investment firms are located. The daily financial dealings on Wall Street affect the national and world economies.

Job Description

Securities sales representatives buy and sell stocks, bonds, and other financial products for clients who wish to invest in such products. They explain investment terms to their clients and the advantages and disadvantages of the investments. Financial service sales representatives usually work for banks and contact potential customers to sell their banking services.

Working Conditions

Securities sales representatives work in hectic offices. Most work 40-hour weeks and many meet with customers on evenings and weekends. Financial services sales representatives work in comfortable, less stressful office environments.

Subjects to Study

Mathematics, English, speech, accounting, economics

Discover More

Check the business section of the newspaper. Find the stock market listings and have a parent or teacher explain them to you. Listen to the stock market report on the nightly news.

Related Jobs

Insurance agents and real estate agents

Earnings	Education and Training	Job Outlook

Average	Bachelor's	Increasing

Services Sales Representatives

Job Description

Services sales representatives sell different services. A hotel sales representative contacts organizations to get convention business. A telephone sales representative sells communication services to businesses. They act as problem solvers in selling their service.

Working Conditions

Some services sales representatives travel for weeks at a time. They may be able to set their own schedules, so long as they meet their company's goals. Others are in their office every day. Competition is stressful, especially at the end of the month when quotas must be met. Prizes are often awarded to those who make the most sales.

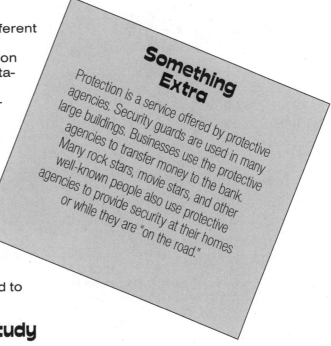

Something Extra

Protection is a service offered by protective agencies. Security guards are used in many large buildings. Businesses use the protective agencies to transfer money to the bank. Many rock stars, movie stars, and other well-known people also use protective agencies to provide security at their homes or while they are "on the road."

Subjects to Study

Mathematics, English, communication skills, business, economics

Discover More

Participate in a fundraising project for an organization or your school. Do you enjoy selling? Are prizes awarded to the sales workers? Why are prizes awarded?

Related Jobs

Real estate agents, insurance agents, securities and financial services sales representatives, manufacturers' and wholesale sales representatives, travel agents

Earnings	Education and Training	Job Outlook
Average	Bachelor's	Increasing

Travel Agents

Something Extra

Where is Timbuktu? What country is also a continent? What state is the home of the Kennedy Space Center? Where is Plymouth Rock? Geography is an important part of a travel agent's knowledge. Travel agents need to be knowledgeable about various locations to get clients to their destinations.

Job Description

Travel agents make travel arrangements such as hotel, airline, car rental, and cruise reservations. They plan group tours and conferences. They advise clients about official papers needed to travel in foreign countries, such as visas and passports. They may also advise on weather conditions, restaurants, and tourist attractions. Computers assist these workers in obtaining the most recent travel information.

Working Conditions

Travel agents work at desks and in front of computer terminals. They talk with clients, do paperwork, and make telephone calls to airlines and hotels. Vacation season can be hectic. Some work long hours. They may travel to hotels, resorts, and restaurants to check their quality.

Subjects to Study

Communication skills, computer skills, geography, foreign languages, history, mathematics, business, accounting

Discover More

Learn more about geography. Several geography computer games are available. Read about various countries and states.

Related Jobs

Secretaries, tour guides, airline reservation agents, rental car agents, travel counselors

Earnings	Education and Training	Job Outlook

Very low-low	Specialized training	Increasing rapidly

Administrative Support Occupations, Including Clerical

Adjusters, Investigators, and Collectors

Job Description

Claim investigators work for insurance companies. They determine the amount of loss and whether the client's policy covers the loss. Then they authorize payments. Adjusters answer customers' questions and complaints about merchandise, service, and billing. They work for banks, stores, and other organizations selling products or services. Collectors notify customers of overdue, unpaid bills by letter and telephone and make arrangements for payment.

Something Extra

Collectors often try to collect bills from debtors over the telephone. Systems connected to computers allow the computer to dial the debtor's telephone number. The collector begins to speak when the connection is made by the computer. This process helps eliminate busy signals and unanswered phones, thereby speeding up the collection process.

Working Conditions

Claim investigators and collectors work in offices and typically work a standard 5-day, 40-hour week. Adjusters often travel to the damaged property or site of the loss. In the case of a disaster, adjusters may be away from home for several days. Dealing with upset or angry clients is part of these jobs, which often causes stress.

Subjects to Study

Mathematics, English, computer skills, economics, business, accounting, foreign language

Discover More

Ask your parents if they have ever filed a claim on their car, home, life, or medical insurance. Find out what they did to file the claim. Did an adjuster contact them?

Related Jobs

Cost estimators, budget analysts, private investigators, auditing and reservation clerks, title searchers, human services workers, financial aid counselors, probation officers

Earnings	Education and Training	Job Outlook

Low	Specialized training/Bachelor's	Increasing

Bank Tellers

Job Description

Bank tellers cash checks, make account deposits and withdrawals, and accept loan payments. In most banks, they use computer terminals to record deposits, withdrawals, and payments. They begin work before the bank opens by counting the cash in their drawer and end the workday by balancing the day's account. Tellers are responsible for making sure the cash in their drawer balances accurately with the day's receipts.

Something Extra

Most banks now have automated teller machines (ATMs) for their customers to use. Customers can take out cash, make loan payments, and make deposits through ATMs. The biggest plus of ATMs is that they are available 24 hours a day, 7 days a week. However, many people still prefer the personal touch of a human teller.

Working Conditions

Tellers work regular 8-hour days Monday through Friday, although some evening and weekend work is required. Many tellers work part-time hours. These workers must pay a high level of attention to security because they work around a lot of money. The ability to communicate well with customers is also important in this job.

Subjects to Study

Mathematics, English, communication skills, computer skills, foreign language, accounting, bookkeeping, economics, public speaking

Discover More

Open a savings or checking account. Ask the teller to explain how to make deposits and withdrawals and use the ATM. Observe the work the teller does when helping you.

Related Jobs

New accounts clerks, cashiers, toll collectors, post office clerks, auction clerks, ticket sellers

Earnings	Education and Training	Job Outlook
Very low	Specialized training/High school	Decreasing

Clerical Supervisors and Managers

Job Description

Clerical supervisors and managers make sure that their staffs are working efficiently. If equipment needs repair or supplies need to be ordered, they ensure that the proper people are notified. They train new employees, plan employees' work, and check progress. They evaluate employees' work habits and hire and fire employees.

Working Conditions

Clerical supervisors and managers work in clean, comfortable offices. Most work 40 hours a week. In organizations that operate 24 hours a day, they may work in shifts including evenings, weekends, and holidays.

Subjects to Study

English, computer skills, business, mathematics, speech

Discover More

Take charge of a class project and assign different parts of the project to different people. Check the progress of the project and notice how each person works.

Related Jobs

Accounting clerks, cashiers, bank tellers, telephone operators, managers

Earnings	Education and Training	Job Outlook

Average	Associate/Bachelor's	Little change

Computer and Peripheral Equipment Operators

Job Description

Computer and peripheral equipment operators oversee computer hardware systems, ensuring that these expensive machines work efficiently. They watch for possible computer problems and try to avoid them. They set controls on the computer and load it with tapes, paper, and disks as needed. If a computer error occurs, they must locate and solve the problem.

Working Conditions

Computer and peripheral equipment operators usually work in comfortable rooms. Because many organizations use their computers 24 hours a day, these workers may be required to work evening or night shifts and weekends, or be on call.

Something Extra

Automation in the computer room has led to many changes in this occupation. Software and robotics allow computers to perform many routine tasks that once were done by computer and peripheral equipment operators. This has caused a decline in the number of workers needed in this occupation.

Subjects to Study

Mathematics, English, communication skills, computer science, physics

Discover More

Learn more about computers and peripheral equipment. Check the library for computer magazines.

Related Jobs

Computer scientists and systems analysts, programmers, computer service technicians, data entry keyers, secretaries, typists, word processors, typesetters, compositors

Earnings	Education and Training	Job Outlook
Low-average	Bachelor's	Decreasing

Credit Clerks and Authorizers

Something Extra

A credit history, which is kept by a credit bureau, shows how an individual pays debts throughout his or her lifetime. It shows the type of loans or credit cards an individual has or had in the past. It tracks whether he or she paid bills on time and how much was paid. It also reveals how much debt a person presently has.

Job Description

Credit clerks collect and verify information needed to obtain credit. If information in an application is questioned, such as employment or financial information, they do further investigating. Credit authorizers research a customer's credit records and decide whether the customer has enough credit available to make a purchase.

Working Conditions

Credit clerks and authorizers usually work 35 to 40 hours a week, although they may work overtime during busy times. These workers may spend a lot of time using video display terminals, which can cause eyestrain and headaches.

Subjects to Study

English, communication skills, computer skills, mathematics

Discover More

Ask your parents if they know what information is in their credit histories. What credit cards do they have? Find out if they have house or car loans and how much they owe on them.

Related Jobs

Claim examiners and adjusters, customer-complaint clerks, procurement clerks, probate clerks, collection clerks

Earnings	Education and Training	Job Outlook

Low	Specialized training/High school	Little change

General Office Clerks

Job Description

General office clerks fill the needs of employers in all kinds of businesses, from doctors' offices to large financial institutions to small wholesalers. Because the needs of their employers can change from day to day, so can their duties. Common duties include filing, typing, keeping payroll records, preparing mailings, and proofreading. Senior office clerks may be responsible for supervising lower level clerks.

Working Conditions

General office clerks usually work a standard 40-hour week in comfortable offices. They may work evening or weekend shifts or overtime. Many clerks work part-time or as temporaries.

Something Extra

An entry-level job, such as that of general office clerk, requires less education and work experience than other positions in a company. People often take entry-level jobs to become established in a certain company. As these employees gain experience and show good work habits, they are often promoted to higher level positions. For example, some presidents of large, international companies started as mailroom clerks or secretaries.

Subjects to Study

English, typing, word processing, keyboarding, computer skills, mathematics, office practices

Discover More

Typing properly is important in this job and in many others. Learn how to type by taking a computer typing program or keyboarding class.

Related Jobs

Cashiers, medical assistants, teacher aides, food and beverage workers

Earnings	Education and Training	Job Outlook

Low	High school	Little change

Information Clerks

Something Extra

The telephone is essential to the work of information clerks. The invention of the telephone was the result of Alexander Graham Bell's attempt to find a way to communicate with the deaf. Often with early telephones voices could not be understood, but the basic idea was correct. People were impressed by the new invention, but few realized that it would one day be a part of nearly every household.

Job Description

Information clerks work for organizations gathering information from individuals or answering questions they have about services or products. Hotel clerks, receptionists, airline reservation agents, and travel clerks are different types of information clerks. These workers answer telephones, greet visitors, and assist customers. They use multiline telephones, fax machines, and computers in their work.

Working Conditions

Information clerks who greet visitors usually work in highly visible, attractive offices. Reservation agents may work in offices shared by several agents. Most work 40-hour weeks, although many jobs require evening, weekend, and overtime work. These jobs may be tiring, repetitive, and stressful—answering a continuously ringing phone all day, for example.

Subjects to Study

English, speech, computer skills, foreign language

Discover More

Learn how to answer the telephone properly and speak clearly into the receiver. Practice recording messages for other members of your family.

Related Jobs

Dispatchers, security guards, bank tellers, guides, telephone operators

Earnings	Education and Training	Job Outlook

Low	High school/Specialized training	Increasing

Hotel and Motel Desk Clerks

Job Description

Hotel and motel desk clerks register guests and assign rooms using computers. They answer guests' questions about the community and the establishment. They keep records of room assignments and collect payments from guests. In smaller establishments, desk clerks may also act as bookkeepers and switchboard operators.

Working Conditions

Hotel and motel desk clerks usually work behind desks in the estab-lishment's lobby area and must stand most of the time. They may work evenings, late nights, weekends, and holidays. More than one in five clerks works part-time.

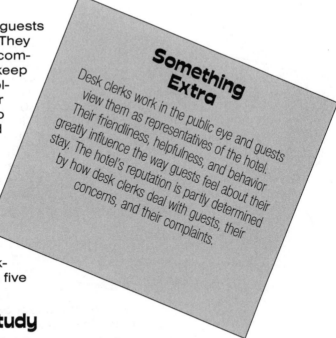

Something Extra

Desk clerks work in the public eye and guests view them as representatives of the hotel. Their friendliness, helpfulness, and behavior greatly influence the way guests feel about their stay. The hotel's reputation is partly determined by how desk clerks deal with guests, their concerns, and their complaints.

Subjects to Study

Mathematics, English, geography, U.S. history, psychology, communication skills, speech, typing, computer skills, foreign language

Discover More

If you were a desk clerk at a hotel or motel in your community, what sites or events would you tell a guest to visit? Which restaurants would you recommend? Make a visitor's guide for your community.

Related Jobs

Dispatchers, security guards, bank tellers, guides, telephone operators

Earnings	Education and Training	Job Outlook
Very low	High school/Specialized training	Increasing

Interviewing and New Accounts Clerks

Job Description

Interviewing and new accounts clerks help people fill out bank account or charge card applications or complete consumer surveys in person, on the telephone, or by mail. Some interviewing clerks gather information needed for admitting patients to a hospital. They may verify information or create files. These workers are also known as customer service representatives.

Working Conditions

New accounts clerks work mostly in bank offices, while clerks who admit patients work in hospitals or doctors' offices. Clerks who conduct surveys usually spend most of their time on the telephone. Many of these workers work part-time. This type of work can be very repetitious.

Something Extra

Surveys are taken for many different reasons, but mostly because companies want to know the buying habits of consumers for marketing information. Some surveys are done by political parties interested in voters' opinions. Interviewing clerks ask people survey questions, carefully record their responses, and send the results to whoever requested the survey.

Subjects to Study

English, spelling, typing, communication skills, mathematics, psychology, foreign language

Discover More

Learn how to fill out applications correctly and neatly. Practice on forms when you enroll in school or join an organization.

Related Jobs

Dispatchers, security guards, bank tellers, guides, telephone operators

Earnings	Education and Training	Job Outlook

Very low	High school	Little change

Receptionists

Job Description

Receptionists greet customers on the phone and at the office and refer them to the proper person or department. Making a good first impression is an important part of this job since this is the first person most customers or clients meet. This job requires the use of personal computers, fax machines, and multiline telephone systems.

Working Conditions

Receptionists sit at desks located in highly visible areas and work a standard 40-hour week. About half of these workers are employed in doctors' offices, hospitals, nursing homes, and health clinics. Many spend their days answering a continuously ringing telephone.

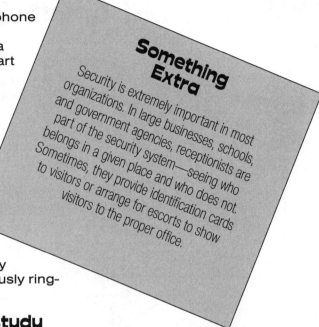

Something Extra

Security is extremely important in most organizations. In large businesses, schools, and government agencies, receptionists are part of the security system—seeing who belongs in a given place and who does not. Sometimes, they provide identification cards to visitors or arrange for escorts to show visitors to the proper office.

Subjects to Study

English, communication skills, spelling, speech, typing, computer skills, psychology

Discover More

Volunteer to be a greeter for a school function such as a play, sports event, or dance. Help anyone who has questions or concerns. How do you feel about being in the public eye?

Related Jobs

Dispatchers, security guards, bank tellers, guides, telephone operators

Earnings	Education and Training	Job Outlook
Very low	High school	Increasing

Reservation and Transportation Ticket Agents and Travel Clerks

Job Description

Reservation and transportation ticket agents make and confirm transportation and hotel reservations, answer questions about rates and routes, and sell tickets. Travel clerks plan trips and offer travel suggestions. They indicate points of interests, quality hotels, and good restaurants to their clients.

Working Conditions

Reservation agents work in large offices with computer terminals. Ticket agents work in airports and other transportation terminals aiding passengers in boarding. Travel clerks work in motor clubs, hotels, and businesses. Meeting preset reservation quotas can make these jobs stressful.

Subjects to Study

English, mathematics, geography, communication skills, computer skills, foreign language

Discover More

Look through the advertisements in travel magazines or the newspaper. Choose a place you would like to visit and send for information about this place.

Related Jobs

Dispatchers, security guards, bank tellers, guides, telephone operators

Earnings	Education and Training	Job Outlook

Low	High school/Specialized training	Increasing

Mail Clerks and Messengers

Job Description

Mail clerks sort and deliver incoming mail to employees in large organizations. They prepare mailing materials to be delivered outside of the organization by folding and inserting them into envelopes and affixing postage. Messengers pick up and deliver letters and packages which need to be sent or received in a hurry between businesses. They may drive, walk, or ride bicycles. Many work for courier services.

Working Conditions

Most mail clerks work regular 40-hour weeks in mailrooms in office buildings. They are often on their feet and may lift heavy loads. Messengers work alone making deliveries in all kinds of weather and traffic, and may work evenings and weekends. Some are paid according to the number of deliveries they make and distance traveled.

Something Extra

Robots are used in some large office buildings to deliver mail from one department to another. As the robot travels on a track through the building, mail is taken from or placed on it. Office workers often become attached to this mechanical friend and give it a special endearing name.

Subjects to Study

Computer skills, communication skills, driver education, geography, English, mathematics, physical education

Discover More

Only electronic facsimile (FAX) machines can deliver copies faster than messengers. However, because original documents are often required in business transactions, a FAX copy often cannot be used. Find out how a FAX machine operates and observe how an original document differs from a faxed one.

Related Jobs

Postal clerks, mail carriers, route drivers, traffic, shipping, and receiving clerks, correspondence review clerks, vault workers, parcel post clerks, reconsignment clerks

Earnings	Education and Training	Job Outlook

Very low	High school	Little change

Material Recording, Scheduling, Dispatching, and Distributing Workers

Job Description

Material recording, scheduling, dispatching, and distributing workers coordinate and keep track of orders for personnel, equipment, and materials. When orders arrive at businesses, clerks unpack, verify, and record incoming merchandise. Dispatchers often work for police or fire stations and handle calls from people reporting emergencies.

Working Conditions

Work in these occupations can be hectic or physically demanding. Most work a regular 40-hour week, although some work evenings, weekends, and holidays. These workers may work in offices or warehouses, inside or outside. Some, such as dispatchers, sit in front of a computer while others stand, lift, and walk most of the day.

Subjects to Study

Mathematics, computer skills, keyboarding, English, physical education

Discover More

Keeping an inventory of materials requires organization. Make an inventory of the materials you use at school. Check any items that you need to restock.

Related Jobs

Airline-radio operators, airline dispatchers, air traffic controllers, stock clerks, material clerks, distributing clerks, routing clerks

Earnings	Education and Training	Job Outlook

Very low	High school	Little change

Dispatchers

Job Description

Dispatchers receive emergency calls, determine the location and seriousness of emergencies, and send police, firefighters, or ambulances to the scene of the emergencies. Other dispatchers, such as those in transportation, coordinate arrivals and departures of shipments to meet specific time schedules. All dispatchers keep records of the calls they receive and the actions they take.

Working Conditions

Dispatchers sit for long periods of time using telephones, computers, and two-way radios. They must remain calm if callers become hysterical or abusive. Evening, weekend, and holiday work is common. Shift work is frequently a part of this job.

Something Extra

During an emergency, a dispatcher must calm the caller to get accurate information so that the needed help is sent to the correct location. The dispatcher sometimes gives first aid instruction to the caller until help arrives. It is important that dispatchers keep in touch with the emergency units until they reach the scene.

Subjects to Study

English, writing skills, computer skills, keyboarding, communication skills

Discover More

Learn how to contact emergency help in your community. Observe a dispatcher in a fire or police department in your community.

Related Jobs

Airline-radio operators, airline dispatchers, air traffic controllers, radio and television transmitter operators, telephone operators, customer service representatives, transportation agents

Earnings	Education and Training	Job Outlook
Low	High school	Little change

Stock Clerks

Something Extra

An inventory consists of all the products a business has available for sale. Keeping an accurate record of its inventory is important to a business for success. Bar coding is used in some businesses to keep the inventory up-to-date. Bar codes are the black stripes you find on items you buy. Stock clerks use hand-held scanners connected to computers to keep the inventory records.

Job Description

Stock clerks receive, unpack, and check materials into the stockroom. They keep records of items entering and leaving the stockroom and report damaged or spoiled goods. They bring items to the sales floor and stock shelves.

Working Conditions

Stock clerks work in warehouses, stock rooms, and shipping and receiving rooms that may not be air-conditioned or heated. Most work a 40-hour week, which may include evenings and weekends. The majority of these workers are employed by department or grocery stores. Overtime may be required during the holiday shopping season. This type of work is physically demanding.

Subjects to Study

English, mathematics, computer skills, physical education

Discover More

Visit a warehouse-style store. Are there any stock clerks working on the floor? If so, notice how they are organizing the goods on the shelves.

Related Jobs

Shipping and receiving clerks, distributing clerks, routing clerks, stock supervisors, cargo checkers

Earnings	Education and Training	Job Outlook

Very low	High school	Little change

Traffic, Shipping, and Receiving Clerks

Job Description

Traffic clerks keep records of all freight coming in and leaving the company and make sure that the charges are correct. Shipping clerks keep records on all outgoing shipments. They fill orders from the stockroom and direct the loading for shipment. Receiving clerks check materials coming into the warehouse, make sure they are in good condition, and route them to the proper department.

Something Extra

The technology of automation has changed the way warehouses operate. Conveyer belts operated by computers, robots, and computer-directed trucks move materials through the buildings much faster than a person can. The use of hand-held computer scanners speeds up the process of receiving goods.

Working Conditions

These clerks work in storage rooms which may not be heated or air-conditioned or they may work outside. Eight-hour days are normal, and evening and weekend hours are often part of this job. These workers must lift and carry heavy or bulky boxes.

Subjects to Study

Mathematics, computer skills, English, business, keyboarding

Discover More

Make a list of basic everyday items that you use, such as toothpaste, tissues, soap, and shampoo. Check your personal inventory. What items need to be restocked?

Related Jobs

Stock clerks, material clerks, distributing clerks, routing clerks, express clerks, expediters, order fillers

Earnings	Education and Training	Job Outlook
Very low	High school	Little change

Postal Clerks and Mail Carriers

Something Extra

Optical character readers (OCRs) and bar code sorters have lessened the mail sorting duties of postal clerks and mail carriers in recent years. These methods are also much faster than using clerks and carriers in the sorting process. The OCRs "read" the zip code and spray a bar code on the mail. Then the mail is sorted using this bar code.

Job Description

Postal clerks sort mail for delivery, sell stamps, weigh packages, and help customers file claims for damaged packages. Mail carriers deliver the mail to homes and businesses on foot or by car and pick up mail from homes and businesses on their route.

Working Conditions

Postal clerks work in clean, well-lighted buildings. They are usually on their feet, lifting and carrying packages and sacks. Some deal with the public during regular working days; others work nights or weekends moving and sorting mail. Mail carriers begin work early in the morning and finish in the afternoon. Some carriers walk while others drive, but all must deliver the mail in every type of weather.

Subjects to Study

English, mathematics, physical education, driver education

Discover More

Find out who delivers your mail and talk to your mail carrier about his or her job. Does your carrier walk or drive? What are the working hours? What does he or she like or dislike about the job?

Related Jobs

Mail clerks, file clerks, routing clerks, sorters, material moving equipment operators, clerk typists, cashiers, data entry operators, ticket sellers, messengers, merchandise deliverers, delivery-route truck drivers

Earnings	Education and Training	Job Outlook

Average	High school	Increasing rapidly

Record Clerks

Job Description

Record clerks are responsible for a variety of business records, including billing and financial information, customer orders, and employee files. In a small business, one clerk may handle all of these duties. Large businesses often hire specialized clerks, such as billing, brokerage, and filing clerks, to work in various areas.

Working Conditions

Record clerks work in offices and may sit for long periods of time. Most work regular 40-hour weeks. Because these workers frequently use video display terminals, they may experience eyestrain, backaches, and headaches.

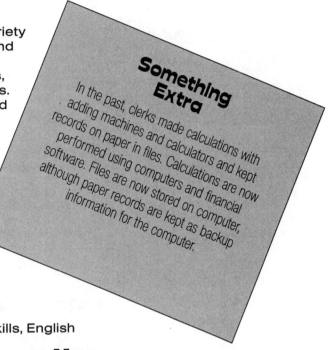

Something Extra

In the past, clerks made calculations with adding machines and calculators and kept records on paper in files. Calculations are now performed using computers and financial software. Files are now stored on computer, although paper records are kept as backup information for the computer.

Subjects to Study

Mathematics, computer skills, office skills, English

Discover More

Talk to your parents about their financial records. How do they keep track of bills that are due? How do they know what bills have been paid? Does someone assume the role of record clerk in your home?

Related Jobs

Bank tellers, statistical clerks, receiving clerks, medical record clerks, hotel and motel clerks, credit clerks, reservation and transportation ticket agents

Earnings	Education and Training	Job Outlook
Low	High school	Little change

Billing Clerks

Something Extra

Many businesses these days are replacing billing machines with computers and specialized billing software. Using computers, clerks are able to calculate the charges and prepare bills in one step. Billing clerks still enter the information and check for accuracy before the bill is printed.

Job Description

Billing clerks keep records of customers' charges and payments. They calculate the total amount due from a customer and prepare an itemized bill explaining the charges. Billing machine operators print out bills and invoices, which are then sent to customers.

Working Conditions

Billing clerks work mainly in offices and spend most of their time at their desks working on computers. Most work a regular 40-hour week, although some put in overtime hours during the holiday season.

Subjects to Study

Mathematics, computer skills, office skills, English

Discover More

Look at the bills mailed to your home. What information is included on each bill? Learn what terms such as transaction date and closing date mean.

Related Jobs

Bank tellers, statistical clerks, receiving clerks, medical record clerks, hotel and motel clerks, credit clerks, reservation and transportation ticket agents

Earnings	Education and Training	Job Outlook

Low	High school	Little change

Bookkeeping, Accounting, and Auditing Clerks

Job Description

Bookkeeping and accounting clerks record the money spent and received by their company. They prepare reports for managers, post bank deposits, and make sure bills are paid. Auditing clerks check the records of other employees in an organization and correct any errors in the records.

Working Conditions

Bookkeeping, accounting, and auditing clerks work in offices and sit for long periods of time. Most work regular 8-hour days, Monday through Friday. They may work longer hours during tax time, at the end of the year, or during audits.

Something Extra

Accurate bookkeeping is essential to a business. Knowing how money is being spent and made helps the manager of a business make decisions about the growth of the company. In case of a tax audit, accurate financial records are required to verify the company's tax payments.

Subjects to Study

Mathematics, office skills, computer skills, English

Discover More

Keep your own financial records. Use a notebook to record any money you receive from allowance, gifts, etc., and then record how you spend that money. Keep any receipts or banking records in a file.

Related Jobs

Bank tellers, statistical clerks, receiving clerks, medical record clerks, hotel and motel clerks, credit clerks, reservation and transportation ticket agents

Earnings	Education and Training	Job Outlook
Low	High school	Little change

Brokerage Clerks and Statement Clerks

Something Extra

A small but growing number of banks no longer return canceled checks to their customers. Only the account statement is sent, and copies of the checks are kept on file at the bank. This process, which is called check truncation, reduces labor and mailing costs for the banks.

Job Description

Brokerage clerks are responsible for records of the sale and purchase of stocks, bonds, and other investments. Statement clerks provide bank customers with statements of their bank accounts each month through the operation of high speed machines. These machines fold the statement and place it in an envelope with canceled checks. This is then mailed to the bank customer.

Working Conditions

Brokerage and statement clerks work in office settings during regular weekday business hours.
Brokerage clerks also work in offices but may put in overtime if activity in the stock market is high.

Subjects to Study

Mathematics, office skills, computer skills, English

Discover More

Ask your parents to show you their checking account monthly statement. Notice the information that is given to the customer. Did your parents receive canceled checks with the statement?

Related Jobs

Bank tellers, statistical clerks, receiving clerks, medical record clerks, hotel and motel clerks, credit clerks, reservation and transportation clerks

Earnings	Education and Training	Job Outlook

Low	High school/Bachelor's	Little change

File Clerks

File clerks classify, store, retrieve, and up-date office information in records which are easily located. They examine incoming information and mark it with a number or letter code. They store the information in a paper file or enter the information in another type of storage device, such as a computer file.

Working Conditions

File clerks work in offices during regular weekday business hours. They spend a lot of time on their feet and must frequently bend, reach, and stoop. About one in every three file clerks works part-time.

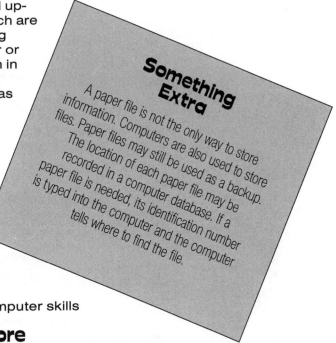

Something Extra

A paper file is not the only way to store information. Computers are also used to store files. Paper files may still be used as a backup. The location of each paper file may be recorded in a computer database. If a paper file is needed, its identification number is typed into the computer and the computer tells where to find the file.

Subjects to Study

English, office skills, keyboarding, computer skills

Discover More

Ask your parents to help you organize your school, activities and sports, and financial information in a filing system at your house. Add to and take away from your files as needed.

Related Jobs

Bank tellers, statistical clerks, receiving clerks, medical record clerks, hotel and motel clerks, credit clerks, reservation and transportation clerks

Earnings	Education and Training	Job Outlook

Very low	High school	Little change

Library Assistants and Bookmobile Drivers

Job Description

Library assistants lend and collect books, issue library cards, and repair books. They provide special assistance to people who can't see well. Bookmobile drivers drive vans or trucks stocked with books to different locations in the community, such as hospitals, nursing homes, and schools. They lend and collect books, collect fines, and act as link between the library and the community.

Working Conditions

Library assistants work in comfortable, quiet libraries behind desks or in the book stacks. Bookmobile drivers work out of automobiles and travel in all kinds of weather. They may be responsible for maintaining the bookmobile. Both types of workers may work evenings and weekends.

Subjects to Study

English, mathematics, computer skills, office skills, driver education

Discover More

Visit a bookmobile in your community and talk to the driver about this job. Ask the driver what kinds of places the bookmobile serves. Observe the people visiting the bookmobile and the types of books they check out.

Related Jobs

Bank tellers, statistical clerks, receiving clerks, medical record clerks, hotel and motel clerks, credit clerks, reservation and transportation ticket agents

Earnings	Education and Training	Job Outlook

Very low	High school	Little change

Order Clerks

Job Description

Order clerks receive and fill requests for such items as machine parts, movie rentals, and clothing. They take the order and send it to the proper department. Orders may come from other employees inside the business, salespeople, or customers outside the business. Most orders are received over the telephone, although some come by mail or fax.

Working Conditions

Many order clerks work in offices at video display terminals with telephones. These workers sit most of the day. Headaches, back strain, and eyestrain may be part of this job. During the holidays or other peak periods when sales are high, overtime work is often required.

Something Extra

More than half of all order clerks work in wholesale or retail sales. Many of these work in catalog sales, in which orders are received by mail, fax, or telephone. The order clerk checks the order to avoid mistakes and calculates the total bill. The order is then sent to the warehouse to be filled.

Subjects to Study

Mathematics, English, computer skills, office skills

Discover More

Look through a catalog and read the directions for placing an order. Fill out the order form with prices of things in the catalog you would like to buy. Figure out what your order would cost, including tax and shipping charges.

Related Jobs

Bank tellers, statistical clerks, receiving clerks, medical records clerks, hotel and motel clerks, credit clerks, reservation and transportation ticket agents

Earnings	Education and Training	Job Outlook
Low	High school	Little change

Payroll and Timekeeping Clerks

Job Description

Payroll and timekeeping clerks make sure that employees receive their paychecks on time and that the checks are for the correct amount. Timekeeping clerks collect timecards from employees and check for errors. Payroll clerks figure an employee's pay by adding up the hours worked and subtracting taxes, insurance, and other deductions.

Working Conditions

Payroll and timekeeping clerks work in offices during regular weekday business hours. Much of their time is spent sitting at desks doing paperwork or working on a computer.

Subjects to Study

Mathematics, office skills, computer skills, English

Discover More

Ask a parent to show you his or her paycheck stub. Notice the difference between the "gross" and "net" earnings. Find out what costs (such as insurance, taxes, and savings plans) are taken from the paycheck. These are called "deductions."

Related Jobs

Bank tellers, statistical clerks, receiving clerks, medical records clerks, hotel and motel clerks, credit clerks, reservation and transportation ticket agents

Earnings	Education and Training	Job Outlook

Low	High school	Decreasing

Personnel Clerks

Job Description

Personnel clerks work with people who are applying for jobs with their organization as well as with newly hired employees. They explain company rules, dress codes, pay policies, and benefits. They also maintain employee records and notify employees of job openings in the company.

Working Conditions

Personnel clerks work in offices during regular weekday business hours. They spend much of their time making telephone calls, writing letters, and updating employee and applicant files. Most work for government agencies, schools, hospitals, and banks.

Something Extra

Companies that perform government work must be concerned with security. Identification clerks keep records on employees of the company. They may check into a new employee's past jobs, schooling, and credit and criminal history. They prepare identification badges for employees and visitors.

Subjects to Study

English, speech, communication skills, office skills, computer skills

Discover More

Get a job application from a business and look at the type of information requested on the form. If you can't get an application from a business, check the library for books with examples of job applications.

Related Jobs

Bank tellers, statistical clerks, receiving clerks, medical records clerks, hotel and motel clerks, credit clerks, reservation and transportation ticket agents

Earnings	Education and Training	Job Outlook
Very low	High school	Little change

Secretaries

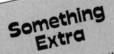

Something Extra

The keys on the first typewriters were arranged in alphabetical order, but this caused problems because the metal bars kept getting stuck together. After researching the letters used most in English, Christopher Sholes, a newspaper editor, created the QWERTY keyboard. It was named for the first six letters on the top line of today's modern typewriters and keyboards.

Job Description

Secretaries have a variety of duties which help keep offices organized. They schedule appointments, maintain files, type correspondence, greet visitors, and answer telephone calls. They work with office equipment such as computer programs, fax machines, and copiers to provide information needed to keep the business running smoothly. Some, such as medical and legal secretaries, do highly specialized work.

Working Conditions

Secretaries work at desks in offices. Because they type a lot on typewriters and computers, eyestrain, backache, wrist and hand problems, and stress are common. They usually work between 35 and 40 hours a week.

Subjects to Study

English, spelling, grammar, speech, keyboarding, computer skills, office skills, mathematics

Discover More

Talk to secretaries at your school or at offices you visit about their training and job duties. Develop some office skills such as keyboarding, filing, and word processing.

Related Jobs

Bookkeepers, receptionists, stenographers, personnel clerks, typists, word processors, legal assistants, medical assistants, systems managers, office managers, human resource officers

Earnings	Education and Training	Job Outlook

Low	High school/Associate	Little change

Stenographers and Court Reporters

Job Description

Stenographers and court reporters put spoken words into written form. Stenographers make notes using shorthand or a stenotype machine, which prints shorthand. The notes are then typed up for use. Court reporters record all statements made during official court or government proceedings. They record statements at speeds of up to 200 words per minute. Because they are the only ones recording the proceedings, accuracy is vital.

Something Extra

Stenotype machines linked to computers are used to help the deaf or hearing-impaired enjoy television programs through closed captioning. This is called "Computer-Aided Transcription." People who want this option install a special decoding device on their televisions that prints the words out on the screen.

Working Conditions

Stenographers work in offices while court reporters usually work in courtrooms or legislatures. They work standard 40-hour weeks, although many court reporters freelance their services and are self-employed. The pressure to be both fast and accurate is often stressful.

Subjects to Study

English, stenographic skills, word processing, spelling

Discover More

Watch an actual court case on television. Find the court reporter in the courtroom and watch what he or she does. Listen to all the statements made by the lawyers, witnesses, and judge and try to imagine correctly recording every word that is spoken.

Related Jobs

Bookkeepers, receptionists, secretaries, personnel clerks, administrative assistants, medical assistants

Earnings	Education and Training	Job Outlook
Low	Specialized training	Decreasing

Teacher Aides

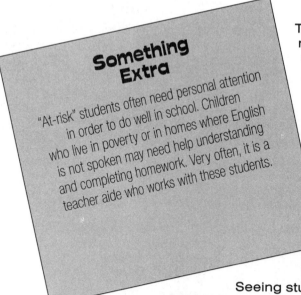

Something Extra

"At-risk" students often need personal attention in order to do well in school. Children who live in poverty or in homes where English is not spoken may need help understanding and completing homework. Very often, it is a teacher aide who works with these students.

Job Description

Teacher aides help children in the classroom and cafeteria or on the playground and field trips. They provide extra attention to some individual students or small groups. They help teachers by grading papers, keeping attendance records, typing, filing, ordering supplies, operating audiovisual equipment, or preparing class lessons.

Working Conditions

Most teacher aides work part-time during the school year in classrooms, although they may work outdoors during recess or field trips. They spend much of their time standing, walking, or kneeling. Seeing students grow and learn can be rewarding, although working closely with students can also be tiring and stressful.

Subjects to Study

English, communication skills, office skills, computer skills, mathematics, foreign language

Discover More

Find out if you can help younger children at school, church, daycare centers, or in a youth organization. Follow the instructions of the person in charge.

Related Jobs

Childcare workers, family daycare providers, library technicians, library assistants

Earnings	Education and Training	Job Outlook

Very low	High school/Associate	Increasing rapidly

Telephone Operators

Job Description

Telephone operators help customers when calls cannot be dialed directly, such as person-to-person or collect calls. They give customers refunds when calls are not made properly. They help handle emergency calls and provide local and long distance telephone numbers.

Working Conditions

Telephone operators work day, evening, or night shifts even on weekends and holidays. Some operators work split shifts, which means they work during the busiest morning and evening times with a few hours off in the afternoon. Pressure to be quick and polite in a closely supervised work environment and with angry or rude customers can be stressful.

Something Extra

Advances in automation have changed basic telephone usage. Often, operators are no longer needed to assist with collect, person-to-person, or overseas calls because computers can handle these tasks. When a long distance call is made, the cost is automatically recorded in the computer for billing. If a telephone number has been changed, a computerized message gives the new number to callers.

Subjects to Study

English, business mathematics, speech, foreign language, office skills, listening skills

Discover More

Do you have good listening skills? Learn to follow directions from teachers and take accurate notes and messages. Find out the difference between active and passive listening.

Related Jobs

Customer service representatives, dispatchers, hotel clerks, information clerks, police aides, receptionists, reservation agents, travel clerks

Earnings	Education and Training	Job Outlook
Low	High school/Specialized training	Decreasing

Typists, Word Processors, and Data Entry Keyers

Something Extra

Working as a typist, word processor, or data entry keyer can cause health problems. The continual use of certain types of office equipment such as computers may cause muscle strain, eye problems, and stress. Some of these workers even develop a painful condition of the hands and wrists known as carpal tunnel syndrome, which can make them unable to work.

Job Description

Typists and word processors set up and type reports, letters, and mailing labels. They may have other office duties as well, such as filing, answering telephones, and sorting mail. Data entry keyers fill out forms that appear on computer screens or enter lists of items or numbers. They may also proofread and edit information.

Working Conditions

Most typists, word processors, and data entry keyers work in clean, comfortable offices and usually sit for long periods of time. Some must contend with high noise levels made by office machines such as printers. Most work from 37 to 40 hours a week.

Subjects to Study

English, office skills, keyboarding, spelling, punctuation, grammar

Discover More

Try to increase your typing or keyboarding speed or learn to type if you don't know how. Use self-help materials such as books, records, or computer programs.

Related Jobs

Stenographers, court reporters, dispatchers, telephone operators

Earnings	Education and Training	Job Outlook

Very low	High school	Little change

Service
Occupations

Correction Officers

Something Extra

In the late 1700s England used its colony of Australia as a prison. Convicted prisoners boarded ships in England and were shipped to Australia, 12,000 miles from their homeland. Some believed that the island country was connected to China and died trying to walk to freedom. Others tried to escape through a sea route and were never heard from again.

Job Description

Correction officers guard people who have been arrested and are awaiting trial and prisoners who have been convicted of crimes. They keep order and enforce rules in jails or prisons and assign and supervise inmates' work. They help inmates with personal problems, supervise them, and report any bad behavior. To prevent escapes, they staff security positions in towers and at gates.

Working Conditions

Correction officers work indoors in varying types of conditions and outdoors in guard towers or prison yards. Most work 8-hour days, 5 days a week. They work weekends, nights, and holidays and overtime is often required. Most correction officers work in large institutions located in rural areas, but some work in jails located in cities and towns. Dealing with convicted criminals is frequently dangerous and stressful.

Subjects to Study

Physical education, driver education, psychology, sociology

Discover More

Some correctional institutions such as state prisons give tours. Check to see if you can visit one to learn more about this occupation.

Related Jobs

Bailiffs, bodyguards, house or store detectives, security guards, police officers, deputy sheriffs, probation and parole officers, recreation leaders

Earnings	Education and Training	Job Outlook

Average	High school/Specialized training	Increasing rapidly

Firefighters

Job Description

Firefighters protect the public from the dangers of fires, and therefore must stay physically fit. At the scene of a fire, they are assigned a particular task and work as part of a team. They rescue victims, perform emergency medical aid, operate equipment, and maintain equipment so that it works properly. Educating the public about fire prevention and safety measures is an important part of this job.

Working Conditions

Firefighters spend much of their time at fire stations where sleeping and dining areas are provided. Most work 50 hours a week or more. When a fire alarm sounds, they must respond regardless of the time or weather. Firefighting is one of the most dangerous occupations because it involves the risk of injury and death.

Something Extra

Fire lookouts locate forest fires from remote lookout stations and report their findings to headquarters by telephone or radio. When fires break out in forests, firefighters go in to battle the blaze. They sometimes parachute into the area of the fire when they are unable to reach it any other way.

Subjects to Study

Physical science, chemistry, driver education, physical education

Discover More

Visit a fire station in your area. Talk to the firefighters about their jobs, required training, and risks involved.

Related Jobs

Fire-protection engineers, police officers, emergency medical technicians

Earnings	Education and Training	Job Outlook
Average	High school/Specialized training	Increasing

Guards

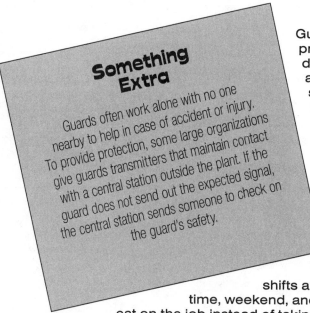

Something Extra

Guards often work alone with no one nearby to help in case of accident or injury. To provide protection, some large organizations give guards transmitters that maintain contact with a central station outside the plant. If the guard does not send out the expected signal, the central station sends someone to check on the guard's safety.

Job Description

Guards, also called security officers, protect property from fire, theft, vandalism, and break-ins. They patrol the area by walking, using a car or motor scooter, or checking individuals entering or leaving the area. At events involving large groups, they provide information and control the crowd. Guards usually wear uniforms and may carry a nightstick or gun.

Working Conditions

Guards work indoors at guard desks or outdoors patrolling the area and may work alone at night. They usually work 8-hour shifts and some rotate shifts to divide daytime, weekend, and holiday work equally. Guards often eat on the job instead of taking meal breaks.

Subjects to Study

English, driver education, physical education, communication skills, computer skills

Discover More

Observe different types of guards when you are shopping, attending public events, and visiting museums. Notice how the guards work with the public and if they carry guns or nightsticks.

Related Jobs

Bailiffs, border guards, correction officers, deputy sheriffs, fish and game wardens, house or store detectives, police officers, private investigators

Earnings	Education and Training	Job Outlook
Very low	High school	Increasing rapidly

Police, Detectives, and Special Agents

Job Description

Police, detectives, and special agents provide protection throughout the nation. State police officers patrol highways, issue traffic tickets, and help accident victims. Detectives and special agents collect evidence and investigate crimes. These workers frequently testify in court about cases in which they are involved.

Working Conditions

Police, detectives, and special agents work 40-hour weeks, but paid overtime work is common. Some evening, night, and holiday work is often required. These workers may work outdoors in all types of weather or indoors at a desk. Police work is dangerous and this can be stressful for the worker as well as his or her family.

Something Extra

Special agents who work for the Federal Bureau of Investigation (FBI) investigate federal crimes including bank robberies, kidnapping, drug smuggling, and spying. During the 1920s and 1930s, the FBI became well-known for battling gangsters and enforcing prohibition laws, which outlawed the sale and use of alcohol.

Subjects to Study

English, psychology, American history, sociology, chemistry, physics, driver education, physical education, foreign language

Discover More

Police departments are interested in keeping close contact with the community. Visit a police station or talk to officers who visit your school.

Related Jobs

Guards, bailiffs, correction officers, deputy sheriffs, fire marshals, fish and game wardens, U.S. marshals

Earnings	Education and Training	Job Outlook
Average	Specialized training/Bachelor's	Decreasing

Chefs, Cooks, and Other Kitchen Service Workers

Job Description

Chefs and cooks prepare meals that are served in restaurants, schools, cafeterias, and hospitals. They may supervise a staff of workers, order food supplies, and plan menus. Kitchen workers do less skilled tasks such as cleaning vegetables, measuring ingredients, and stirring soups and sauces. They are also responsible for keeping the kitchen clean and washing dishes.

Something Extra

Can food influence one person to love another? Through the ages some common foods have been thought of as "love potions." Honey was recommended by Hippocrates, the father of medicine. One common saying about food and love is, "The way to a man's heart is through his stomach."

Working Conditions

Kitchen workers often work in crowded, hectic, and hot areas, especially during peak dining times. Lifting heavy pots and standing for long periods of time can be tiring. In restaurants, evening, holiday, and weekend work is normal, while hours in schools and other institutions are more regular. Part-time work is common.

Subjects to Study

Mathematics, home economics, nutrition, vocational education

Discover More

Plan a menu for your family for one week. Choose foods that are both nutritious and appetizing. Remember to include items from each of the four food groups.

Related Jobs

Butchers and meatcutters, cannery workers, industrial bakers

Earnings	Education and Training	Job Outlook

Very low	High school	Increasing

Food and Beverage Service Workers

Job Description

Food and beverage service workers deal with customers directly. Waiters and waitresses take food orders, serve food, prepare the bill, and accept payment. Bartenders fill customers' drink orders. Hosts and hostesses welcome diners and show them to their tables. Other workers clean dirty tables and reset the tables with silverware and napkins.

Working Conditions

Food and beverage service workers spend most working hours on their feet. They carry heavy trays and must serve customers quickly and courteously during busy times. Evening, weekend, and holiday work is common. This occupation employs more part-time workers than almost all others.

Something Extra

Many high school students work at fast food restaurants part time after school and on weekends. To encourage young people to apply for work, some fast food restaurants offer college scholarships to student workers. For many young people, these jobs provide money for the present but they don't view them as careers.

Subjects to Study

Mathematics, communication skills, speech, English, foreign language

Discover More

Talk to a friend or older sibling who has worked in a fast food restaurant. Find out what they liked and disliked about the job. What hours and days did they work?

Related Jobs

Flight attendants, butlers, tour bus drivers

Earnings	Education and Training	Job Outlook
Very low	High school	Little change

Dental Assistants

Job Description

Dental assistants help dentists with patient care, office duties, and laboratory duties. They assist the dentist during patient examinations and treatment. They also schedule appointments, maintain patient records, handle billing, and order supplies. Those with laboratory duties clean removable dental devices and make temporary crowns for teeth.

Working Conditions

Dental assistants work in very clean environments. They wear gloves and masks to protect themselves and their patients from diseases and germs. Most of their work is done standing or sitting near the dental chair. They work 32 to 40 hours each week, including some Saturdays and evenings.

Subjects to Study

Biology, chemistry, health, office skills, computer skills, communication skills

Discover More

Learn how to care for your own teeth to prevent cavities. If you are unsure of the correct methods, ask the dental assistant to show you how to brush and floss your teeth properly.

Related Jobs

Medical assistants, physical therapy assistants, occupational therapy assistants, pharmacy assistants, veterinary technicians

Earnings	Education and Training	Job Outlook

Very low	Specialized training	Increasing

Medical Assistants

Job Description

Medical assistants perform routine tasks to keep doctors' offices running smoothly. They answer phones, greet patients, schedule appointments, arrange for hospital admissions, handle billing, and file patient records. They may take medical histories, explain treatments to patients, and help doctors with examinations.

Working Conditions

Medical assistants work in comfortable, clean offices, where they are in constant contact with other people. Because many of these people do not feel well, courtesy and compassion are important. Most work 40-hour weeks, including some evenings and weekends. These workers may handle several responsibilities at once during busy times.

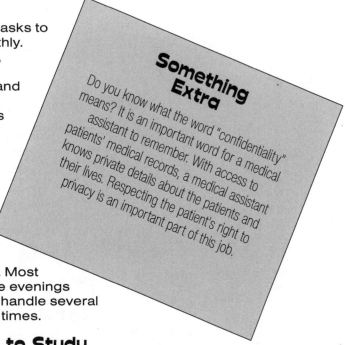

Something Extra

Do you know what the word "confidentiality" means? It is an important word for a medical assistant to remember. With access to patients' medical records, a medical assistant knows private details about the patients and their lives. Respecting the patient's right to privacy is an important part of this job.

Subjects to Study

Mathematics, health, biology, typing, bookkeeping, computer skills, office skills

Discover More

To learn more about what these workers do, try taking care of someone in your home who gets sick. Make the person who doesn't feel well comfortable and bring juice, soup, or medicine to his or her bedside.

Related Jobs

Medical secretaries, hospital admitting clerks, pharmacy helpers, medical record clerks, dental assistants, occupational therapy aides, physical therapy aides

Earnings	Education and Training	Job Outlook
Very low	High school	Increasing rapidly

Nursing Aides and Psychiatric Aides

Job Description

Nursing aides and psychiatric aides care for patients in hospitals, nursing homes, and mental health settings. They feed, bathe, and dress patients, help patients in and out of bed, take temperatures and blood pressures, and set up equipment. They observe patients and report any signs or changes that might be important for the doctors or nurses to know.

Something Extra

Aides in nursing homes and mental health residences often have more contact with patients than other staff members. Because these patients often spend months or years in these homes, aides often build relationships with them. Many patients see aides as special friends, and a caring aide can greatly influence a patient's attitude and outlook on life.

Working Conditions

Aides work about 40 hours a week, including some evening, weekend, and holiday work. They must guard against injury when lifting and moving patients. Their duties are not always pleasant and may include emptying bed pans and dealing with irritable or violent patients.

Subjects to Study

Nutrition, anatomy, communication skills, nursing aide training

Discover More

To learn more about this occupation, volunteer to help at a nursing home, hospital, or mental health facility. Some of these places hire students to interact with the patients.

Related Jobs

Homemaker-home health aides, childcare attendants, companions, occupational therapy aides, physical therapy aides

Earnings	Education and Training	Job Outlook

Very low	Specialized training	Increasing

Animal Caretakers, Except Farm

Job Description

Animal caretakers feed, water, bathe, and exercise animals. They play with the animals, observe them for illness or injury, and clean and repair their cages. Kennel staff care for pets such as cats and dogs; stable workers groom, exercise, and care for horses; and zookeepers care for wild and exotic animals.

Working Conditions

Animal caretakers may work outdoors in all kinds of weather. Some of their work is unpleasant, such as cleaning cages or killing hopelessly diseased or aged animals. They may be exposed to bites, kicks, or diseases from animals. Working hours are irregular, including some weekends or nights. Some travel with animals to sports events or shows.

Something Extra

Feeding the animals in a zoo can be a real challenge. Zookeepers must know the type of food each animal needs as well as how much and how often. They must also be careful when feeding dangerous animals such as lions and tigers. Exotic animals may need special foods that must be specially ordered or grown.

Subjects to Study

Mathematics, life sciences, zoology, biology, communications skills, chemistry

Discover More

Animal shelters and zoos often need volunteers. Learn about this occupation by becoming a volunteer.

Related Jobs

Agricultural and biological scientists, veterinarians, retail sales workers in pet stores, gamekeepers, game-farm helpers, poultry breeders, ranchers, artificial-breeding technicians

Earnings	Education and Training	Job Outlook
Very low	High school/Specialized training	Increasing

Barbers and Cosmetologists

Job Description

Barbers and cosmetologists help people look their best. They cut, trim, shampoo, and style hair. Other services they provide include coloring, perming, or straightening hair; fitting hairpieces; shaving male customers; and giving facial massages and advice on makeup. Many cosmetologists are also trained to give manicures. They also keep customer records and order supplies.

Working Conditions

The work of barbers and cosmetologists is performed while standing, and they are often exposed to chemicals. Working evenings and weekends is normal in this occupation. Some work more than 40 hours a week, although one out of three works part-time. Many own their own businesses.

Subjects to Study

Communication skills, mathematics, business, speech, health

Discover More

Practice styling your hair or someone else's. Look at some hairstyling magazines for ideas and styles. Barber and cosmetology schools in your area may offer tours.

Related Jobs

Instructors, beauty supply distributors, manicurists, makeup artists

Earnings	Education and Training	Job Outlook

Very low	High school/Specialized training	Increasing

Preschool Workers

Job Description

While parents are working, going to school, or away for other reasons, preschool workers care for children five years old and younger. They care for basic needs such as feeding, changing diapers, and keeping the children safe and comfortable. They organize activities that help the children socialize and learn, and communicate with parents about their children.

Working Conditions

Preschools are located in family homes, schools, churches, daycare centers, and workplaces. While the work is rewarding, it can be tiring to care for the needs of each child. Some preschools are open nine or ten months of the year; others are open year-round. Workers in daycare centers may work in shifts because of parents' work schedules.

Something Extra

Play is a child's work; it is how preschool-aged children learn. Playing house, school, or grocery store is actually a learning activity. Art and music activities allow children to explore their talents and be creative. Playing with other children teaches them how to share, socialize, and gain independence from their parents.

Subjects to Study

English, communication skills, child development, psychology, home economics, art, music, drama, health, speech

Discover More

Visit a preschool and talk with the workers and children. What type of training do the workers have? The easiest way to learn about this job is to babysit or help someone else take care of preschoolers.

Related Jobs

Teacher aides, children's tutors, kindergarten and elementary school teachers, early childhood program directors, child psychologists

Earnings	Education and Training	Job Outlook

Very low-low	High school/Associate	Increasing rapidly

Flight Attendants

Job Description

Flight attendants are responsible for the safety and comfort of airline passengers. Their most important duty is helping passengers in an emergency. They also stock the plane with food, drinks, blankets, first aid kits, and other supplies. During the flight, they serve food and drinks and assist passengers who need help or information. They may administer first aid to passengers who become ill.

Working Conditions

Flight attendants are away from their homes and families much of the time. Many work evenings, nights, and holidays. Dealing with demanding passengers, flying in severe weather, and serving meals quickly on short flights can be stressful. Flight attendants must remain efficient and calm even during emergencies.

Subjects to Study

English, communication skills, foreign language, speech, first aid, health, physical education

Discover More

To learn more about this occupation, observe a flight attendant working the next time you fly on a plane. You may also be able to talk to a flight attendant by visiting an airport.

Related Jobs

Emergency medical technicians, firefighters, maritime crews, camp counselors

Earnings	Education and Training	Job Outlook

Very low-low	Specialized training/Bachelor's	Increasing rapidly

Gardeners and Groundskeepers

Job Description

Gardeners and groundskeepers care for lawns, trees, gardens, and other plant life and keep the grounds free of litter. Gardeners prune, feed, and water gardens and mow and water lawns at private homes and public places. Groundskeepers maintain athletic fields, golf courses, cemeteries, and parks. They also mow, water, and fertilize the grounds.

Something Extra

Many gardeners in the United States are self-employed. Being self-employed means an individual must attract customers who will use his or her services. He or she must handle the billing for the work completed, supervise any employees, and be responsible for all work that is done.

Working Conditions

Gardeners and groundskeepers work outside in all types of weather. Much of this work is seasonal, mainly in the spring and summer. They may be pressured to complete their work, especially when preparing for scheduled events such as sports competitions. These workers must be careful with the chemicals and dangerous equipment they use.

Subjects to Study

Biology, zoology, botany, driver education, mathematics

Discover More

Plant a garden or some flowers around your home. If you don't have a yard, plant seeds in soil in a pot. Feed and water the planted seeds and growing plants.

Related Jobs

Construction workers, landscape architects, nursery workers, farmers, horticultural workers, tree surgeon helpers, tree trimmers, pruners, forest conservation workers

Earnings	Education and Training	Job Outlook
Very low	High school/Specialized training	Increasing

Homemaker-Home Health Aides

Job Description

Homemaker-home health aides allow elderly, disabled, and seriously ill patients to live at home instead of in a nursing home or hospital. They clean, do laundry, prepare meals, and help with a patient's personal hygiene. They also check the patient's pulse and blood pressure and give medication. Aides keep records of each patient's condition and progress.

Something Extra

Animals are sometimes used as companions for the elderly. Both monkeys and dogs have been used to help disabled individuals. These trained animals help with simple household tasks, provide protection, and get items for their human friends. Their owners enjoy more independence.

Working Conditions

Homemaker-home health aides often work part-time, and weekend hours are common. They may work in homes that are clean or dirty, pleasant or depressing. Patients may be cooperative or difficult. Many aides work for agencies and are assigned to certain patients. They may go to the same home every day for months or years or visit several homes each day.

Subjects to Study

Home economics, nutrition, health, first aid, English, mathematics

Discover More

Do you know an elderly person or relative who has a homemaker-home health aid? By talking to the aide, you can learn more about this occupation.

Related Jobs

Attendants in children's institutions, childcare attendants in schools, child monitors, companions, nursing aides, nursery school attendants, occupational therapy aides, physical therapy aides, playroom attendants, psychiatric aides

Earnings	Education and Training	Job Outlook

Very low	High school/Specialized training	Increasing rapidly

Janitors and Cleaners and Cleaning Supervisors

Job Description

Janitors, cleaners, and cleaning supervisors keep offices, schools, hospitals, hotels, and other public buildings clean and in good condition. They do such varied jobs as cleaning, repairing, emptying trash, painting, and mowing lawns. Cleaning supervisors assign tasks, supervise employees, and order supplies.

Working Conditions

Janitors and cleaners often work evenings, while school and hospital custodians work days. Most work about 40 hours a week. Work is done both inside and outside. Dirty work such as cleaning bathrooms and trash containers is part of this job. These workers spend most of their time on their feet, sometimes lifting and pushing heavy furniture or equipment.

Something Extra

Technology, which has affected many jobs, is not expected to have a great effect on this occupation. Robots are being developed to perform cleaning tasks, but most can only do one task. They are not practical for use in small areas such as hospital or hotel rooms.

Subjects to Study

Mathematics, shop courses, communication skills

Discover More

Observe the janitor in your school. List all the chores and different tasks that he or she does.

Related Jobs

Refuse collectors, floor waxers, street sweepers, window cleaners, gardeners, boiler tenders, pest controllers, general maintenance repairers

Earnings	Education and Training	Job Outlook
Very low	High school	Little change

Private Household Workers

Job Description

Private household workers clean homes, care for children, cook meals, and do laundry. They may be companions for the elderly or disabled. Childcare workers may be responsible for a child's physical needs and education. Housekeepers, butlers, caretakers, and cooks are other private household workers.

Working Conditions

Private household workers work in homes or apartments owned by wealthy employers. They sometimes interact with other workers, but they are often the only employee in the home. Most work days and return home at night. Some live in a private room in the home, and these workers' hours may be longer. Some employers can be very demanding.

Subjects to Study

Home economics, childcare, first aid, cooking, shop courses

Discover More

Talk to your neighbors about caring for their children. For a few hours of work, you may earn a small amount of cash and learn what it is like to be in charge of a household.

Related Jobs

Building custodians, hotel and restaurant cleaners, childcare workers in daycare centers, home health aides, cooks, kitchen workers, waiters and waitresses, bartenders

Earnings	Education and Training	Job Outlook

Very low	High school	Increasing

Agriculture, Forestry, Fishing and Related Occupations

Farm Operators and Managers

Job Description

American farm operators and managers produce enough food to meet the needs of our nation and to export large quantities to other countries. Farm operators may own or rent land and employ farm managers to oversee the farm's functions. Crop farms require planting, maintaining, and harvesting. Livestock, dairy, and poultry farms require caring for and breeding the animals and repairing farm buildings.

Working Conditions

Farm operators and managers work from dawn to dusk during the planting and harvesting seasons. Because work on crop farms may last only six or seven months each year, these workers often have second jobs. Work on livestock or dairy farms is constant because chores need to be done every day. Machinery, animals, and chemicals make farm work dangerous.

Subjects to Study

Mathematics, computer skills, mechanics, agriculture, life science, business, shop courses

Discover More

Check into programs such as Future Farmers of America (FFA) or 4-H clubs in your community. These organizations offer excellent training in farm-related work.

Related Jobs

Agricultural engineers, animal breeders, animal scientists, county agricultural agents, dairy scientists, extension service specialists, feed and farm management advisors, horticulturists, plant breeders, poultry scientists

Earnings	Education and Training	Job Outlook

Very low-average	Specialized training/Bachelor's	Decreasing

Fishers, Hunters, and Trappers

Job Description

Fishers catch fish and other water life for human food, animal feed, and other uses. Hunters track and kill animals for government agencies or money. They may hunt alone, with others, or with dogs. Trappers catch animals using traps or cages and sometimes sell wild animal skins. Live animals may be caught for animal control or research.

Working Conditions

Fishers, hunters, and trappers work under dangerous conditions where help may not be easily available. The hours are often long, and strenuous physical outdoor work is part of these jobs. Fishers may spend weeks at sea. Hunters and trappers may walk long distances in rough terrain.

Something Extra

Live animals are sometimes trapped for relocation if they are causing problems. For example, bears near a campground are dangerous to campers. Beavers and muskrats sometimes build dens that disrupt the flow of water in a stream. Animals with rabies must also be trapped and destroyed to protect other animals and humans from the disease.

Subjects to Study

Physical education, mechanics, business, mathematics

Discover More

Learn about living in the outdoors. Programs such as Girl Scouts or Boy Scouts teach camping and other outdoor skills.

Related Jobs

Zoo keepers, loggers, animal control officers, forest rangers, fishing guides, fish hatchery and aquaculture workers, game wardens, harbor pilots, merchant marine officers and seamen, wildlife management specialists

Earnings	Education and Training	Job Outlook
Average	Specialized training	Decreasing

Forestry and Logging Workers

Something Extra

The logging industry has its own special language or jargon. Using chain saws, *fallers* and *buckers* cut down trees, remove the branches, and cut the logs into specified lengths. *Choker setters* fasten chokers (steel chains) around logs to be skidded (dragged) by tractors to the landing. *Riggers* set up and dismantle the cables and guide wires on the logs.

Job Description

Forestry and conservation workers help develop, maintain, and protect forests by planting new trees, fighting insects and diseases that attack trees, and helping to control soil erosion. Timber cutters and loggers cut down thousands of acres of forests each year for timber to be used by industries that produce wood and paper products.

Working Conditions

Forestry and logging workers work outdoors in all types of weather, often in isolated areas. Their work is physically demanding and dangerous. To avoid injury, these workers wear hard hats, eye and hearing protection, safety clothing, and heavy boots.

Subjects to Study

Physical education, first aid, mechanics

Discover More

Learn to identify different types of trees. Study a tree identification book and then visit a forest or park. See how many trees you can identify.

Related Jobs

Arborists, gardeners, groundskeepers, landscapers, nursery workers, range aides, soil conservation technicians

Earnings	Education and Training	Job Outlook

Very low	Specialized training	Decreasing

Mechanics, Installers, and Repairers

Aircraft Mechanics and Engine Specialists

Job Description

Aircraft mechanics and engine specialists inspect various parts of airplanes for mechanical problems. They make needed repairs and test the equipment to make sure it is working properly. Some mechanics work on all different types of aircraft, while others specialize in one part of the aircraft such as the engine or electrical system.

Working Conditions

Aircraft mechanics and engine specialists work in airplane hangars or other indoor areas. They occasionally work outdoors to make quick repairs. They may work under time pressures so that passengers are not inconvenienced by delayed flights. Working in awkward positions, lifting heavy objects, and listening to loud noise are parts of this job. They work 8-hour morning, evening, and night shifts.

Subjects to Study

Mathematics, physics, chemistry, electronics, computer science, mechanical drawing, English

Discover More

To find out more about aircraft mechanics, write to: Aviation Maintenance Foundation, P.O. Box 2826, Redmond, WA 98073.

Related Jobs

Electricians, elevator repairers, telephone maintenance mechanics

Earnings	Education and Training	Job Outlook
Average	High school/Specialized training	Decreasing

Automotive Body Repairers

Job Description

Automotive body repairers restore cars and trucks damaged in accidents, straightening bent bodies, removing dents, and replacing crumpled parts that are beyond repair. They usually receive directions from a supervisor about what parts should be replaced or repaired and how long the job should take. In large shops, they may specialize in one type of repair such as glass installation or door repairing.

Something Extra

Many newer cars have parts that are made of plastic. A body repairer can apply heat from a hot-air welding gun or put the part in hot water to make the plastic soft. The softened part can be molded into its original shape by hand and put back on the car.

Working Conditions

Automotive body repairers work 40 to 60 hours a week inside repair shops. Noise, dust, and paint fumes are part of the work environment. They often work in cramped positions doing strenuous, dirty work. Hazards include cuts from sharp edges, burns from torches, and injuries from power tools.

Subjects to Study

Shop courses, automotive body repair, English, mathematics

Discover More

A model car has many of the same parts as a regular car. Try building a model of a car.

Related Jobs

Automotive and diesel mechanics, automotive repair service estimators, painters, body customizers

Earnings	Education and Training	Job Outlook
Low	High school/Specialized training	Increasing

Automotive Mechanics

Job Description

Automotive mechanics repair and service cars, trucks, and vans with gasoline engines. Mechanics must be able to diagnose the cause of a car's problem quickly and correctly. During routine service, they inspect, adjust, and replace a car's parts. They follow a checklist to be sure they examine any part that could cause a future breakdown.

Working Conditions

Automotive mechanics work 40-hour weeks, but self-employed mechanics may work longer hours. Most work indoors in well-ventilated, noisy repair shops. Mechanics handle dirty parts, lift heavy objects, and work in awkward positions. Minor cuts, burns, and bruises are common, although most serious injuries can be avoided through safety practices.

Subjects to Study

English, mathematics, shop courses, automotive mechanics, electronics, physics, chemistry

Discover More

Find someone you know who works on cars, possibly one of your parents. Ask if you can help. You will learn a lot if you watch and listen while the work is being done.

Related Jobs

Diesel truck and bus mechanics, motorcycle mechanics, automotive body repairers, painters, and customizers, repair service estimators

Earnings	Education and Training	Job Outlook

Low-average	High school/Specialized training	Little change

Diesel Mechanics

Job Description

Diesel mechanics repair and maintain diesel engines in heavy trucks and buses, in farm equipment such as tractors, and in construction equipment such as bulldozers and cranes. Much of their time is spent doing preventive maintenance to assure safe operation, prevent wear and tear to parts, and reduce costly breakdowns.

Working Conditions

Diesel mechanics work indoors, although they occasionally make emergency repairs on the road. They handle greasy parts and may stand or lie in cramped positions to make repairs. Their work area is well-lighted, heated, and ventilated.

Something Extra

Diesel engines are heavier and last longer than gasoline engines. They are also more fuel efficient because a diesel engine compresses the fuel more. This means that a greater amount of fuel is available as power for the vehicle. Diesel engines are used throughout the United States in large trucks, buses, and locomotives.

Subjects to Study

English, mathematics, shop courses, automotive repair, electronics

Discover More

Get some science books at the library. Read about engines and how they work. Find out how gasoline and diesel engines are alike and different.

Related Jobs

Aircraft mechanics, automotive mechanics, boat engine mechanics, farm equipment mechanics, mobile heavy equipment mechanics, motorcycle mechanics, small-engine specialists

Earnings	Education and Training	Job Outlook

Average	Specialized training/Associate	Little change

Electronic Equipment Repairers

Job Description

Electronic equipment repairers install, repair, and maintain electronic equipment such as televisions, computers, telephone systems, and industrial equipment controls. Many work for telephone companies and others work in homes, factories, offices, and hospitals. They keep detailed records of each piece of equipment's repairs and problems.

Working Conditions

Electronic equipment repairers work in shifts, including weekends and holidays, and may be on call for emergencies. Their work involves physical activity such as lifting and moving heavy objects. They must take safety precautions to protect against work hazards such as burns or electrical shock.

Subjects to Study

Mathematics, physics, shop courses, electricity, electronics

Discover More

When your family has some electronic equipment repaired, visit the service center. Talk to the repairer about this occupation. Ask how the repairer became interested in this work and what training is needed.

Related Jobs

Appliance and power tool repairers, automotive electricians, broadcast technicians, electronic organ technicians, vending machine repairers, electronic engineering technicians

Earnings	Education and Training	Job Outlook

Average	Specialized training	Decreasing

Commercial and Industrial Electronic Equipment Repairers

Job Description

Commercial and industrial electronic equipment repairers install and repair equipment that controls the production processes in factories. Many repairers are employed by the federal government. They install radar, missile controls, and communication systems on ships, aircraft, tanks, and in buildings.

Working Conditions

Nearly one-third of commercial and industrial electronic equipment repairers work for the federal government, almost all for the Department of Defense in military environments. Others work for telephone companies, hospitals, and repair shops. Most work in comfortable surroundings.

Something Extra

Devices for hurling missiles at enemies have been used by armies for centuries. During the Middle Ages armies launched stones, liquid fire, dead horses, and even manure into their enemies' camps. Gunpowder and the invention of the first guns brought that type of warfare to an end. Weapons are now much more sophisticated and destructive.

Subjects to Study

Mathematics, physics, shop courses, electricity, electronics

Discover More

Science clubs, Scouts, and 4-H Club offer projects in electricity and electronics. Adults who have experience in these fields are often available to help with projects. Check your local area for these opportunities.

Related Jobs

Appliance and power tool repairers, automotive electricians, broadcast technicians, electronic organ technicians, vending machine repairers, electronics engineering technicians

Earnings	Education and Training	Job Outlook
Average	Specialized training	Decreasing

Communications Equipment Mechanics

Something Extra

Digital systems which are used to switch telephone calls are being used by telephone companies. These systems, which use computers and software, require fewer repairs and have self-diagnosing features that allow repairs to be made more quickly. Fewer mechanics are needed as technology becomes more efficient.

Job Description

Communications equipment mechanics install, repair, and maintain complex telephone communications equipment. Most work either in the central office of the telephone company or at the customer's worksite. Communications equipment mechanics may also work on radio equipment, TV cables, or railroad systems.

Working Conditions

Communications equipment mechanics may work in offices, customers' workplaces, or work shops. Most work for telephone companies. Others work for cable television companies, railroads, and airlines.

Subjects to Study

Mathematics, shop courses, electronics, electricity, physics

Discover More

When you have problems with cable television or the telephone, ask the company how the problem is solved. Ask to talk to the person who finds the problem and solves it.

Related Jobs

Appliance and power tool repairers, automotive electricians, broadcast technicians, electronic organ technicians, vending machine repairers, electronics engineering technicians

Earnings	Education and Training	Job Outlook

Average	Specialized training	Decreasing

Computer and Office Machine Repairers

Job Description

Computer repairers install and repair computers, equipment used with computers, and word processing systems. Office machine repairers work on copiers, typewriters, cash registers, and mail processing equipment. Some repairers service both computer and office equipment.

Working Conditions

Computer and office machine repairers may work in offices, shops, or customers' worksites. They usually work in clean, well-lit, air-conditioned surroundings. Many work regular 40-hour weeks, although some may repair equipment during evenings after an office has closed.

Something Extra

Thomas Jefferson, the author of the Declaration of Independence, invented a very simple copying machine. As the writer wrote one copy, a second pen connected to the machine made another copy of the document. This way the writer was able to create two copies with one stroke of the pen.

Subjects to Study

Mathematics, computer science, physics, shop courses, electricity, electronics

Discover More

Have an adult supervise you while you look inside a computer. Learn how to connect the various computer cables to other computer equipment such as a printer.

Related Jobs

Appliance and power tool repairers, automotive electricians, broadcast technicians, electronic organ technicians, vending machine repairers, electronic engineering technicians

Earnings	Education and Training	Job Outlook

Average	Specialized training	Increasing

Electronic Home Entertainment Equipment Repairers

Something Extra

Many electronic home entertainment equipment repairers are self-employed. Keeping correct financial records is important, and collecting bills is part of their job. They must maintain good customer relations so that the business remains open. Being self-employed means providing your own tools, shop or office facilities, and vehicles for traveling.

Job Description

Electronic home entertainment equipment repairers work on radios, televisions, stereos, cameras, video games, and other home electronic equipment. They run tests to find the problem and adjust and replace parts. They may also make recordings and listen to them to detect problems.

Working Conditions

Most repairers work in stores that sell electronic home entertainment equipment, electronics repair shops, or service centers. Most work 40-hour weeks, although weekend or evening hours are often required. Self-employed workers often work longer hours.

Subjects to Study

Mathematics, shop courses, electronics, physics, business

Discover More

Ask the person in charge of the public address system at your school, church, or large auditorium to show you how the system is controlled.

Related Jobs

Appliance and power tool repairers, automotive electricians, broadcast technicians, electronic organ technicians, vending machine repairers, electronics engineering technicians

Earnings	Education and Training	Job Outlook

Average	Specialized training	Decreasing

Telephone Installers and Repairers

Job Description

Telephone installers and repairers work on customers' property installing and repairing telephones and communication equipment. When customers move or request additional phone lines or other services, installers make the changes. They install lines and telephone jacks in new buildings.

Working Conditions

Telephone installers and repairers work at customers' businesses or homes or construction sites. They may work on rooftops, ladders, and telephone poles. Almost all of these workers are employed by telephone companies.

Something Extra

Technology has taken work away from telephone installers. In the past every telephone had to be installed by a professional. Today buildings are prewired with telephone jacks, and customers purchase their own telephones and simply plug them in. Many phones are no longer repaired because it is often less expensive to simply buy a new one.

Subjects to Study

Mathematics, physics, shop courses, electricity, electronics

Discover More

You can find out more about careers in the telephone industry by asking for a copy of *Phonefacts* from: United States Telephone Association, Small Companies Division, 900 19th Street NW, Suite 800, Washington, DC 20006.

Related Jobs

Appliance and power tool repairers, automotive electricians, broadcast technicians, electronic organ technicians, vending machine repairers, electronics engineering technicians

Earnings	Education and Training	Job Outlook

Average	High school/Specialized training	Decreasing

Elevator Installers and Repairers

Something Extra

A dumbwaiter is a small elevator used to move materials from one level to another. Dumbwaiters were sometimes installed in older homes for servants to use. A tray of food prepared in a downstairs kitchen could be delivered to an upstairs bedroom quickly and easily.

Job Description

Elevator installers and repairers assemble, install, and replace elevators and escalators in new and old buildings. They make repairs and modernize older equipment. They test the equipment to make sure it works properly. These workers must have a thorough knowledge of electricity and electronics.

Working Conditions

Elevator installers and repairers work a 40-hour week, but maintenance workers may be on call and required to work overtime. Most of the work is indoors. They work in small spaces, lift and carry heavy equipment, and are exposed to falls and electrical shocks.

Subjects to Study

Mathematics, shop courses, electricity, electronics, physics, first aid

Discover More

To learn more about this occupation, check the telephone book or the library for a local group of the International Union of Elevator Constructors.

Related Jobs

Boilermakers, electricians, industrial machinery repairers, millwrights, sheet-metal workers, structural ironworkers

Earnings	Education and Training	Job Outlook

Average	Specialized training	Little change

Farm Equipment Mechanics

Job Description

Farm equipment mechanics repair all types of farm machinery—tractors, combines, planters, hay balers, irrigation equipment, milking machines, and more. They maintain machinery by tuning, cleaning, and adjusting engines and checking for any problems.

Working Conditions

Farm equipment mechanics mostly work inside repair shops, although they sometimes travel to farms to make emergency repairs. During the busy planting and harvesting seasons, they are kept busy working six or seven days a week. During the winter, they work fewer hours and may be unemployed.

Something Extra

In some parts of the United States, people known as the Amish do not use any mechanical or electrical equipment on their farms. They still use horses to pull farm equipment and till the ground. But even the Amish have experienced the pressures of big farming. In recent years, many have left the farming life to become construction workers.

Subjects to Study

Vocational courses, diesel and gas engines, hydraulics, welding, electronics

Discover More

Visit a farm, a farm equipment show, or a state fair. Check out the equipment used on modern farms.

Related Jobs

Aircraft mechanics, automotive mechanics, diesel mechanics, mobile heavy equipment mechanics

Earnings	Education and Training	Job Outlook

Very low	High school/Specialized training	Little change

General Maintenance Mechanics

Job Description

General maintenance mechanics combine the skills of plumbers, electricians, painters, carpenters, and other workers. They maintain equipment in hospitals, stores, offices, and other businesses. They may do all the repairs in a small organization or be responsible for a specific area in a large business.

Working Conditions

General maintenance mechanics do many different jobs in one day in several buildings or different parts of one building. They may stand for long periods of time, lift heavy objects, and work in hot or cold environments. A 40-hour week is normal, with some evening, night, or weekend work. They must take safety measures to prevent shocks, burns, and falls.

Subjects to Study

Mathematics, shop courses, mechanical drawing, electricity, woodworking, blueprint reading, science

Discover More

Learn how to do simple household repairs and maintenance jobs. Ask your parents if they have the tools and materials needed to make repairs.

Related Jobs

Carpenters, plumbers, industrial machinery mechanics, electricians, air-conditioning, refrigeration, and heating mechanics

Earnings	Education and Training	Job Outlook

Low	High school/Specialized training	Increasing

Heating, Air-Conditioning, and Refrigeration Technicians

Job Description

Heating, air-conditioning, and refrigeration technicians keep us warm or cool by installing and repairing heating systems, air conditioners, and refrigerators. They help keep people comfortable and prevent food and medicine from spoiling. They must be able to maintain, diagnose, and correct problems within the entire system.

Working Conditions

Technicians work in homes, stores, hospitals, factories, and offices. They may work outside in hot or cold weather or inside buildings without heat or air-conditioning. They must follow safety rules to avoid shock and other injuries. Most work 40 hours a week, but are often on call.

Something Extra

Chlorofluorocarbon (CFC) refrigerants are used in air-conditioning and refrigeration systems. When CFCs escape into the atmosphere, they destroy the ozone layer which protects both plants and animals from excessive radiation. If the ozone layer becomes completely destroyed, nothing will survive on our planet. Technicians use care to conserve, recover, and recycle CFCs.

Subjects to Study

Shop courses, mathematics, electronics, mechanical drawing, applied physics and chemistry, blueprint reading, physical education

Discover More

Talk to someone in the frozen food and dairy section of a local supermarket. Ask what is done when this equipment needs to be repaired.

Related Jobs

Boilermakers, electrical appliance servicers, electricians, plumbers, pipefitters, sheetmetal workers

Earnings	Education and Training	Job Outlook
Low	High school/Specialized training	Increasing

Home Appliance and Power Tool Repairers

Job Description

Home appliance and power tool repairers repair ovens, washers, dryers, refrigerators, and other home appliances as well as power tools such as saws and drills. They find the problem and replace or repair defective parts and tighten, clean, and adjust other parts if needed. Repairers keep records, prepare bills, and collect payments.

Something Extra

Some people enjoy working on their own and do not like having to answer to a supervisor. Home appliance and power tool repairers usually work on their own without a boss. Some people choose this occupation because they enjoy this freedom. Self-employed appliance and tool repairers work from their own workshops. Others may work through appliance and tool stores.

Working Conditions

Repairers work in repair shops and customers' homes and most work a 40-hour week. They sometimes work in cramped and hard-to-reach areas around appliances. They must take safety measures when working around electricity and gas.

Subjects to Study

Shop courses, electricity, electronics, mathematics

Discover More

Talk to a repairer when you take an appliance to the repair shop or when an appliance in your home is being repaired. Find out how he or she learned to make repairs.

Related Jobs

Heating, air-conditioning, and refrigeration mechanics, pinsetter mechanics, office machine and cash register servicers, electronic home entertainment equipment repairers, vending machine servicers and repairers

Earnings	Education and Training	Job Outlook

Low	High school/Specialized training	Little change

Industrial Machinery Repairers

Job Description

Industrial machinery repairers maintain machinery in factories or plants to keep production on schedule. This includes keeping machines and their parts well-oiled, tuned, and cleaned. When repairs must be made, the repairer must work quickly to keep from delaying production and causing the company to lose money.

Working Conditions

Industrial machinery repairers usually work a 40-hour week; however, emergency repairs may be needed at night or on weekends. They may work in cramped areas or on ladders above or beneath machinery. They wear protective gear such as hard hats and protective goggles.

Something Extra

Being able to spot and fix little problems before they cause major breakdowns is important for industrial machinery repairers. If a machine is making a vibration, the mechanic needs to find if the problem comes from worn belts, loose bearings, or another problem. Self-diagnostic systems sometimes alert repairers to potential trouble spots before symptoms develop.

Subjects to Study

Mechanical drawing, mathematics, blueprint reading, physics, electronics, physical education, computer skills

Discover More

Tour a factory and observe the machinery used in production. What would happen in the factory if an important piece of machinery broke down?

Related Jobs

Aircraft mechanics, engine specialists, automotive and motorcycle mechanics, diesel mechanics, elevator installers and repairers, farm equipment mechanics, machinists, general maintenance mechanics, heating, air-conditioning, and refrigeration mechanics, millwrights, mobile heavy equipment mechanics

Earnings	Education and Training	Job Outlook

Average	Specialized training	Little change

Line Installers and Cable Splicers

Something Extra

Fiber optic cables, which are made of tiny strands of glass, are used to replace old copper cables. These cables provide electricity, telephone service, or cable television to homes and businesses. Workers drive to worksites in vans specially designed to be used as workshops. The machinery and materials needed to remove the old cables and install the new ones are inside these mobile workshops.

Job Description

Line installers and cable splicers construct networks of wires and cables used to provide electricity, telephones, and cable television to customers. They check the lines for damage and clear the lines of tree limbs. They make emergency repairs when needed.

Working Conditions

Line installers and cable splicers climb, lift, and often work in cramped or stooped positions. They work outdoors in all kinds of weather and are on call 24 hours a day. During a storm that knocks out power, they may work long, irregular hours. This job is dangerous because they work underground, high above ground, and with chemicals and high voltages of electricity.

Subjects to Study

English, mathematics, physical education, shop courses, electricity

Discover More

The local electric company, telephone company, or cable television company are good sources of information about this occupation.

Related Jobs

Communication equipment mechanics, biomedical equipment technicians, telephone installers and repairers, electricians, sound technicians

Earnings	Education and Training	Job Outlook

Average	High school/Specialized training	Decreasing

Millwrights

Job Description

Millwrights work with machinery and heavy equipment used in almost every industry. They supervise the unloading, inspecting, and moving of equipment at a worksite. They assemble and take apart machinery. They work to maintain machinery to avoid breakdowns.

Working Conditions

Millwrights working in manufacturing work in typical shop settings. Most work 40-hour weeks, although overtime is common during busy production periods. Most wear safety belts, protective glasses, and hard hats. They may work independently or as part of a team. Working quickly and precisely is important to keep production on schedule.

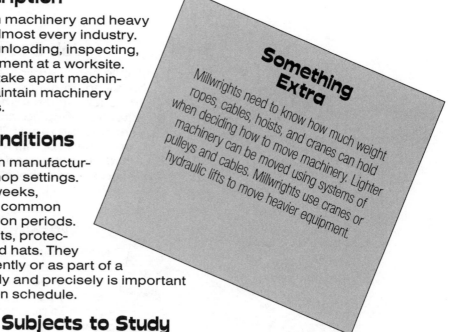

Something Extra

Millwrights need to know how much weight ropes, cables, hoists, and cranes can hold when deciding how to move machinery. Lighter machinery can be moved using systems of pulleys and cables. Millwrights use cranes or hydraulic lifts to move heavier equipment.

Subjects to Study

Science, mathematics, mechanical drawing, machine shop, physical education

Discover More

Use a science book to do some experimenting with pulleys. Try building a pulley that will make a difficult job easier.

Related Jobs

Industrial machinery repairers, mobile heavy equipment mechanics, aircraft mechanics, engine specialists, diesel mechanics, farm equipment mechanics, ironworkers, machine assemblers

Earnings	Education and Training	Job Outlook
Average	High school/Specialized training	Little change

Mobile Heavy Equipment Mechanics

Something Extra

When heavy equipment breaks down at a logging site or a mine, bringing the equipment to a repair shop is too expensive and difficult. For this reason, a field service mechanic in a specially equipped truck travels to the site to make the repair. Many mechanics enjoy the independence of working outside the repair shop.

Job Description

Mobile heavy equipment mechanics repair heavy equipment such as motor graders, trenchers, and backhoes used in construction, logging, and mining. They service and repair diesel engines and other parts of this machinery. Repairing hydraulic lifts used to raise and lower scoops and shovels is an important part of this job.

Working Conditions

Mobile heavy equipment mechanics work in repair shops and outdoors. They lift heavy tools, work with dirty, greasy parts, and often work in cramped positions. Mechanics must be careful to avoid burns, cuts, and bruises from hot engine parts and sharp edges.

Subjects to Study

Mathematics, automobile mechanics, physics, chemistry, English, basic science

Discover More

Observe some heavy equipment being used at a construction site. Talk to a construction worker about what happens when equipment breaks down.

Related Jobs

Railcar repairers, diesel, farm equipment, and mine machinery mechanics

Earnings	Education and Training	Job Outlook

Average	Associate	Little change

Motorcycle, Boat, and Small-Engine Mechanics

Job Description

Motorcycle, boat, and small-engine mechanics repair everything from chain saws to yachts. To make repairs the mechanic usually talks to the owner to try and understand the problem. Testing is done to find the source of the problem. Routine checkups on engines are another part of this job.

Working Conditions

Motorcycle, boat, and small-engine mechanics work in well-lighted, noisy repair shops. Boat mechanics may work outdoors in all weather. In some areas of the country, mechanics work fewer than 40 hours a week in the winter. In warmer weather, working more than 40 hours a week is common.

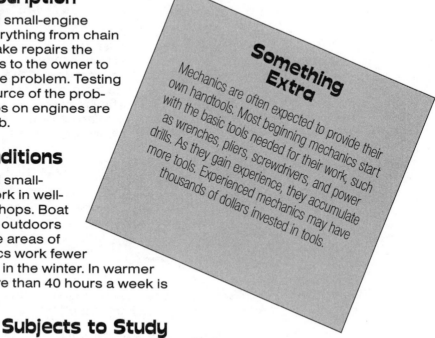

Something Extra

Mechanics are often expected to provide their own handtools. Most beginning mechanics start with the basic tools needed for their work, such as wrenches, pliers, screwdrivers, and power drills. As they gain experience, they accumulate more tools. Experienced mechanics may have thousands of dollars invested in tools.

Subjects to Study

Business arithmetic, small-engine repair, automobile mechanics, science, basic electronics

Discover More

Help someone prepare a lawnmower for spring use or winter storage. Learn about the various parts of the motor.

Related Jobs

Automotive mechanics, diesel mechanics, farm equipment mechanics, mobile heavy equipment mechanics

Earnings	Education and Training	Job Outlook

Low	High school/Specialized training	Little change

Musical Instrument Repairers and Tuners

Job Description

Musical instrument repairers and tuners adjust musical instruments so that they perform properly. To diagnose a problem, they talk to the customer and take the instrument apart to look at parts. They may specialize in working on particular instruments such as pianos, violins, or guitars.

Working Conditions

Musical instrument repairers and tuners working on brass, woodwind, percussion, and string instruments usually work in music stores or repair shops. Piano and organ repairers and tuners work in homes, churches, and schools. They may spend several hours a day driving. Self-employed workers usually work from their homes.

Subjects to Study

Woodworking, instrumental music, communication skills

Discover More

If you have an instrument, try to tune it. Talk to a music teacher or band director about how to care for instruments.

Related Jobs

Electronic home entertainment equipment repairers, vending machine servicers and repairers, home appliance and power tool repairers, computer and office machine repairers

Earnings	Education and Training	Job Outlook

Average	Specialized training	Little change

Vending Machine Servicers and Repairers

Job Description

Vending machine servicers and repairers check coin-operated machines which provide soft drinks, snacks, sandwiches, and other items. They retrieve money, restock the machines, and make sure the machines are clean and working properly. Some paperwork is needed to order parts and keep records of used merchandise.

Working Conditions

Vending machine servicers and repairers spend much time servicing machines in public places where people are gathered.
Work in a repair shop is quiet and not crowded. Because vending machines operate 24 hours a day, these workers may work overtime at night, on weekends or holidays.

Something Extra

Put 50 cents in the slot and you can try your skill at the latest video game. The game will usually last as long as your skill holds out. Vending machines are part of the entertainment industry in our society. Other entertaining vending machines are pinball machines and juke boxes.

Subjects to Study

Driver's education, shop courses, electronics, electricity, machine repairs, English, mathematics

Discover More

Check the newspaper want ad section for business opportunities. Find out if any vending machine opportunities are available.

Related Jobs

Home appliance and power tool repairers, electronic equipment repairers, general maintenance mechanics

Earnings	Education and Training	Job Outlook
 Average	Specialized training	 Little change

Construction Trades
and
Extractive
Occupations

Bricklayers and Stonemasons

Job Description

Bricklayers and stonemasons lay sidewalks and patios, build fireplaces, and install ornamental exteriors on buildings. Bricklayers work with concrete blocks, firebrick linings in furnaces, and brick. Stonemasons work with natural and artificial stone. They often build walls on churches, office buildings, and hotels.

Working Conditions

Bricklayers and stonemasons work outdoors in all types of weather. They stand, kneel, and bend for long periods of time and move heavy materials. Injuries from tools or falls from scaffolding are possible. Many of these workers are self-employed.

Subjects to Study

Mathematics, mechanical drawing, shop courses, sketching

Discover More

Observe the different buildings and other structures made of brick or stone in your community. Is there a certain type of brick or stone that is used often? Why? Look for any pattern that might have been used in putting the structure together.

Related Jobs

Concrete masons, plasterers, terrazzo workers, tilesetters

Earnings	Education and Training	Job Outlook

Low	High school/Specialized training	Little change

Carpenters

Job Description

Carpenters do a variety of construction work—woodworking, concrete work, drywalling, and many other jobs. They replace doors, windows, and locks; make repairs on furniture; hang kitchen cabinets; and install machinery. They work with hand and power tools and read blueprints.

Working Conditions

Carpenters form the largest group of building trade workers. Three out of every four carpenters work in new construction or remodeling. Others are self-employed or work for businesses, government agencies, or schools. Carpenters must stand, kneel, climb, and bend. Falls and injuries from power tools are possible. Outdoor work is common.

Something Extra

In the past, carpentry often was a family trade. Boys were taught by their fathers, who had been taught by their fathers. Skills were handed down from one generation to the next. In Studs Terkel's book, *Working*, Nick Lindsay, a carpenter, began learning his family's trade at age 13. Carpentry has been a part of the Lindsay family history since 1755.

Subjects to Study

General mathematics, shop courses, mechanical drawing, carpentry, first aid

Discover More

Try a simple carpentry project such as building a dog house, shelf, or flower box. First, get a plan and gather the materials you need. Be sure you know how to use any tools safely before you begin.

Related Jobs

Bricklayers, concrete masons, electricians, pipefitters, plasterers, plumbers, stonemasons, terrazzo workers

Earnings	Education and Training	Job Outlook
Low	High school/Specialized training	Little change

Carpet Installers

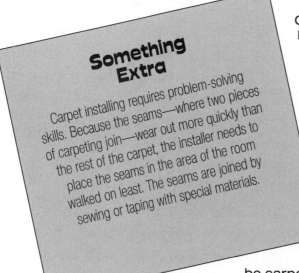

Something Extra

Carpet installing requires problem-solving skills. Because the seams—where two pieces of carpeting join—wear out more quickly than the rest of the carpet, the installer needs to place the seams in the area of the room walked on least. The seams are joined by sewing or taping with special materials.

Job Description

Carpet installers put carpet in new or old buildings and houses. They first check the existing floor for any needed repairs or imperfections. Then they measure the floor and plan the carpet layout. They stretch the carpet to make it fit snugly before they attach it to a stripping, which holds it in place.

Working Conditions

Carpets are installed last in the construction process, so carpet installers work in cleaner, more comfortable areas than other construction workers. Daytime hours are normal; however, businesses may be carpeted in the evening or on weekends. Kneeling, bending, stretching, and lifting heavy carpet rolls are common.

Subjects to Study

General mathematics, shop courses, driver's education

Discover More

Talk to someone in a furniture or carpet store about the way carpet is installed. Look at the carpet in your home or school to see if you can find the seams.

Related Jobs

Carpenters, cement masons, drywall installers, floor layers, lathers, painters, paperhangers, roofers, sheet-metal workers, terrazzo workers, tilesetters

Earnings	Education and Training	Job Outlook

Low	Specialized training	Little change

Concrete Masons and Terrazzo Workers

Job Description

Concrete—a mixture of cement, gravel, sand, and water—is used for home patios, huge dams, and miles of roads. Concrete masons set the concrete and smooth the finished surface. Terrazzo workers add marble chips to the surface of concrete to create decorative walls, sidewalks, and panels.

Working Conditions

Concrete masons and terrazzo workers work outdoors, but work usually stops during rain or freezing weather. These workers must bend and kneel a lot. Kneepads and water-repellent boots are worn for protection.

Something Extra

The ancient Romans took road building quite seriously. Only Roman men of the highest rank were allowed to build and maintain the roads. Twenty-nine roads led from Rome to various parts of the Roman Empire. The roads were so well-constructed that they have lasted for more than 2,000 years.

Subjects to Study

Shop courses, general mathematics, blueprint reading, mechanical drawing, driver's education, physical education

Discover More

Check with your art teacher for materials similar to concrete that are used in craft and art activities. Try completing a project using one of these materials.

Related Jobs

Bricklayers, form builders, marble setters, plasterers, stonemasons, tilesetters

Earnings	Education and Training	Job Outlook

Low	High school/Specialized training	Little change

Drywall Workers and Lathers

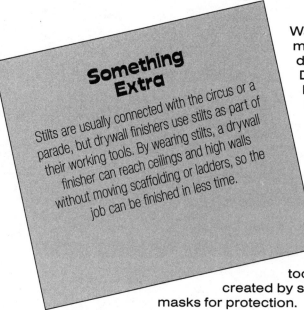

Something Extra

Stilts are usually connected with the circus or a parade, but drywall finishers use stilts as part of their working tools. By wearing stilts, a drywall finisher can reach ceilings and high walls without moving scaffolding or ladders, so the job can be finished in less time.

Job Description

Walls and ceilings in most buildings are made of drywall. Drywall installers fasten drywall panels to a building's framework. Drywall finishers fill the joints between boards and prepare the wall for decorating. Lathers put metal or gypsum lath on walls, ceilings, and frameworks for support.

Working Conditions

Drywall workers and lathers spend much time on their feet, either standing, bending, or kneeling. Most work is done indoors. Workers must be careful around power tools, ladders, and high scaffolding. Dust created by sanding requires these workers to wear masks for protection.

Subjects to Study

Shop courses, carpentry, physical education, basic mathematics

Discover More

Visit a home center or lumberyard to look at some drywall. Find out what tools and supplies drywallers use.

Related Jobs

Carpenters, floor covering installers, form builders, insulation workers, plasterers

Earnings	Education and Training	Job Outlook

Low	High school/Specialized training	Increasing

Electricians

Job Description

The work of electricians provides lights, refrigeration, and electricity in homes. Electricians work with blueprints to install heat, air-conditioning, and other electrical systems. They must follow government rules and building codes when doing their work. They make repairs when breakdowns occur and give advice about the safety of electrical equipment.

Working Conditions

Electricians work 40 hours a week, although overtime may be required. Some work nights, weekends, and are on call. These workers follow strict safety precautions to avoid electrical shock, falls, and cuts. They sometimes work in tight places in awkward or cramped positions.

Something Extra

Did you know that people can produce static electricity? A person walking across a carpet in dry winter weather may build up an electrical charge of several thousand volts. Touching a metal surface may result in a shock. Usually this electricity is released harmlessly through the hair.

Subjects to Study

Mathematics, shop courses, electricity, electronics, mechanical drawing, science, first aid

Discover More

Learn how to be safe around electrical appliances and systems. Check the library for some electrical projects you could try.

Related Jobs

Air-conditioning mechanics, cable installers and repairers, electronics mechanics, elevator constructors

Earnings	Education and Training	Job Outlook
Average	High school/Specialized training	Little change

Glaziers

Job Description

Glaziers select, cut, install, and remove all types of glass and plastic in doors, windows, showers, baths, and other places. For most jobs, the glass is precut and mounted in frames. Large, heavy pieces may be lifted by cranes to be put in place. Once the glass is in place, glaziers secure it with bolts, cement, metal clips, or wood molding.

Working Conditions

Glaziers work outdoors in all types of weather. They lift, bend, kneel, and stand much of the time. Some work requires standing on high scaffolds. Glaziers may be injured by falling, broken glass, or sharp tools, or by improperly lifting heavy glass panels.

Subjects to Study

Basic mathematics, shop courses, blueprint reading, mechanical drawing, general construction, first aid

Discover More

Learn more about different ways to work with glass. Go to an arts and crafts mall and observe someone blowing glass.

Related Jobs

Bricklayers, carpenters, floor layers, paperhangers, terrazzo workers, tilesetters

Earnings	Education and Training	Job Outlook

Low	High school/Specialized training	Increasing

Insulation Workers

Job Description

Insulation is used in buildings to save energy by keeping heat in during the winter and heat out in the summer. Insulation workers cement, staple, wire, tape, or spray insulation. Insulation is often blown into place by a hose or machine.

Working Conditions

Insulation workers usually work indoors. Working on ladders, in tight spaces, and in dusty, dirty areas is common. Small particles of insulation can be irritating to the eyes, skin, and respiratory system. For safety, insulation workers wear protective suits, masks, and respirators, take decontamination showers, and keep their work areas well-ventilated.

Something Extra

Asbestos is a material that was once used to insulate buildings, but it has been found to cause cancer. By law, asbestos must be removed from buildings before they are remodeled or torn down. Before removing it, insulation workers must seal the area. Workers wear protective clothing to prevent contact with the dangerous material.

Subjects to Study

Shop courses, blueprint reading, sheet-metal layout, general construction, physical education, driver's education

Something More

Talk to your parents about the insulation in your home. Some utility companies do energy surveys that help customers make improvements to their homes to save energy. Ask your parents if they have ever had a survey.

Related Jobs

Carpenters, carpet installers, drywall applicators, floor layers, roofers, sheet-metal workers

Earnings	Education and Training	Job Outlook

Low	Specialized training	Increasing rapidly

Painters and Paperhangers

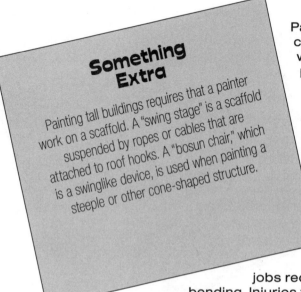

Something Extra

Painting tall buildings requires that a painter work on a scaffold. A "swing stage" is a scaffold suspended by ropes or cables that are attached to roof hooks. A "bosun chair," which is a swinglike device, is used when painting a steeple or other cone-shaped structure.

Job Description

Painters and paperhangers make surfaces clean, attractive, and bright and protect walls exposed to the outdoors. Painters prepare surfaces for painting, mix paints and match colors, and apply various kinds of finishes to structures. Paper-hangers cover walls and ceilings with decorative wall coverings made of paper, vinyl, or fabric.

Working Conditions

Most painters and paperhangers work for contractors engaged in new construction, repair, restora-tion, or remodeling work. They must be physically fit because their jobs require a lot of standing, climbing, and bending. Injuries from falls and working with hazardous materials are part of the dangers of their jobs. Much work is done outdoors but seldom in bad weather.

Subjects to Study

Shop courses, art courses, mathematics, physical education

Discover More

Get permission to paint an old piece of furniture or some other item. Find out what needs to be done before painting the item. Be sure to work in a well-ventilated area.

Related Jobs

Billboard posterers, metal sprayers, undercoaters, transportation equipment painters

Earnings	Education and Training	Job Outlook

Very low	Specialized training	Increasing

Plasterers

Job Description

Plasterers apply plaster to walls and ceilings to make them fire-resistant and more soundproof. Increasingly today, plasterers apply insulation to the outside of new and old buildings. They may create smooth or textured finishes. Skilled plasterers sometimes specialize in complex decorative work.

Working Conditions

Plastering is physically demanding because workers often stand, bend, lift, and reach overhead. Plasterers work both indoors and outdoors. Their work is dusty and dirty, and the materials they use sometimes can be irritating to the eyes and skin.

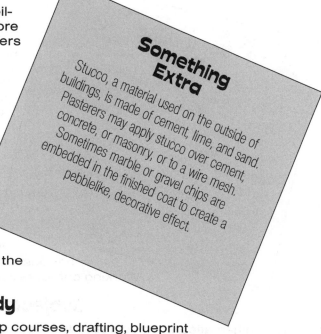

Something Extra

Stucco, a material used on the outside of buildings, is made of cement, lime, and sand. Plasterers may apply stucco over cement, concrete, or masonry, or to a wire mesh. Sometimes marble or gravel chips are embedded in the finished coat to create a pebblelike, decorative effect.

Subjects to Study

Mathematics, mechanical drawing, shop courses, drafting, blueprint reading, physical education

Discover More

Make a plaster of Paris mold. Get some plaster of Paris and follow the directions on the package for mixing. Pour some of the mixture into a styrofoam meat tray. Place some leaves, small shells, and beads on the wet plaster of Paris. After the plaster is dry, remove the styrofoam tray.

Related Jobs

Drywall finishers, bricklayers, concrete masons, marble setters, stonemasons, terrazzo workers, tilesetters

Earnings	Education and Training	Job Outlook
Low	High school/Specialized training	Little change

Plumbers and Pipefitters

Job Description

Plumbers install and repair water, waste disposal, drainage, and gas systems in homes and other buildings. They install showers, sinks, toilets, and appliances. Pipefitters install and repair pipe systems that are used in manufacturing, creating electricity, and heating and cooling buildings.

Working Conditions

Plumbers and pipefitters normally work 40-hour weeks. They may work weekends and nights, or be on call if they are contracted as maintenance workers. They need to be physically strong to lift heavy pipes, stand for long periods, and work in uncomfortable positions. Working outdoors in cold or wet weather is part of this job.

Subjects to Study

General mathematics, shop courses, drafting, blueprint reading, physics

Discover More

Check with your parents about how you can learn to do some simple plumbing repairs in your home. Do-it-yourself guides are available at the library.

Related Jobs

Boilermakers, stationary engineers, electricians, elevator installers, heating, air-conditioning, and refrigeration mechanics, industrial machinery repairers, millwrights, sheet-metal workers

Earnings	Education and Training	Job Outlook

Average	High school/Specialized training	Decreasing

Roofers

Job Description

Roofers install roofs made of tar or asphalt and gravel, rubber, metal, and other materials. Most houses have roofs covered with shingles. Repair and reroofing—replacing old roofs in existing buildings—is another part of this job. Some roofers also waterproof concrete walls and floors.

Working Conditions

Roofers do physically demanding work including lifting, climbing, bending, and kneeling. They risk injury from slips, falls, and burns. In fact, the roofing industry has the highest accident rate of all construction work. Roofers work in all types of weather.

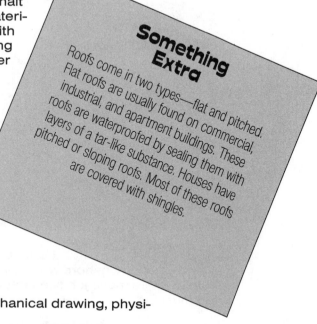

Something Extra

Roofs come in two types—flat and pitched. Flat roofs are usually found on commercial, industrial, and apartment buildings. These roofs are waterproofed by sealing them with layers of a tar-like substance. Houses have pitched or sloping roofs. Most of these roofs are covered with shingles.

Subjects to Study

Basic mathematics, shop courses, mechanical drawing, physical education

Discover More

Look at the different types of roofs in your community. Observe different types of roofs in various buildings. Can you find any houses with roofs that aren't shingled?

Related Jobs

Carpenters, concrete masons, drywall applicators, floor covering installers, plasterers, terrazzo workers, tilesetters

Earnings	Education and Training	Job Outlook
Low	High school/Specialized training	Little change

Roustabouts

Job Description

Roustabouts do physical labor such as digging ditches, loading and unloading trucks, cutting down trees and bushes, and connecting pipes. They work around oil fields, gas facilities, and pipelines and frequently assist skilled workers. Much of their work is done using hand tools such as hammers, wrenches, and shovels.

Working Conditions

Most roustabouts do hard, outdoor work. Some work on offshore drilling platforms where strong ocean storms, tides, and currents occur. They live on the platform, working 12 hours a day for 7 days, and then have 7 days off. Onshore workers work standard 40-hour weeks. Some workers move job sites frequently. Risks include falls, cuts, and strained muscles.

Subjects to Study

Shop courses, welding, electricity, mechanics, mathematics, physical education

Discover More

Learn more about the oil industry and its history. Read about offshore drilling and the environment. Check the library for information.

Related Jobs

Construction laborers, dockhands, material handlers

Earnings	Education and Training	Job Outlook

Average	High school/Specialized training	Decreasing

Sheetmetal Workers

Job Description

Sheetmetal workers use metal sheets to make ductwork for air-conditioning and heating systems. They also make roofs, rain gutters, skylights, outdoor signs, and other products made from sheets of metal. Installing and maintaining the products is part of this job.

Working Conditions

Sheetmetal workers work in shops or at the job site. They usually work a 40-hour week. These workers lift heavy and bulky items and stand for long periods of time. Safety glasses are worn to protect their eyes. Jewelry and loose-fitting clothing cannot be worn around the machinery.

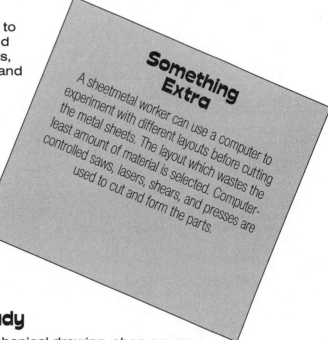

Something Extra

A sheetmetal worker can use a computer to experiment with different layouts before cutting the metal sheets. The layout which wastes the least amount of material is selected. Computer-controlled saws, lasers, shears, and presses are used to cut and form the parts.

Subjects to Study

Algebra, trigonometry, geometry, mechanical drawing, shop courses, physical education

Discover More

To find out more about this occupation, write to: The Sheet Metal National Training Fund, 601 N. Fairfax St., Suite 240, Alexandria, VA 22314.

Related Jobs

Layout workers, machinists, metal fabricators, metal patternmakers, shipfitters, tool and die makers, heating, air-conditioning, and refrigeration technicians, glaziers

Earnings	Education and Training	Job Outlook
Average	High school/Specialized training	Increasing

Structural and Reinforcing Ironworkers

Something Extra

Cranes and other heavy equipment arrive at the construction site in pieces. Before construction can begin, they must be put together and hoisting cables must be set up. Ironworkers use mobile cranes to assemble this machinery, which in turn moves the steel, cement, and other construction materials needed to do their job.

Job Description

Structural and reinforcing ironworkers assemble steel frames used to strengthen bridges, buildings, highways, and other structures. They install metal stairways, window frames, decorative ironwork, and other metal products. Some erect metal storage tanks and premade metal buildings.

Working Conditions

Structural and reinforcing ironworkers work outdoors in all types of weather. Those who work in extremely high places do not work when it is wet, icy, or windy. To avoid injuries from falls, these workers use safety belts, scaffolding, and nets.

Subjects to Study

General mathematics, mechanical drawing, shop courses, metalworking, blueprint reading

Discover More

Bridge construction has changed as transportation has changed. Learn how bridge building has changed in recent decades. Design a bridge using a computer or paper and pencil.

Related Jobs

Operating engineers, concrete masons, welders

Earnings	Education and Training	Job Outlook

Low	High school/Specialized training	Little change

Tilesetters

Job Description

Tilesetters use cement or mastic (a sticky paste) to set tiles on walls, floors, and ceilings. To create a pattern, the tilesetter may arrange the tiles on a dry floor before installing it. When the cement or mastic is dry, the joints between the tiles are filled with grout, which is a very fine cement.

Working Conditions

Tilesetters usually work indoors. Because they perform their work when most of the construction is complete, they work in relatively clean, uncluttered areas. Knee-pads are worn to protect knees. Much of the work day is spent bending, kneeling, and reaching.

Something Extra

In ancient Rome and Egypt, tile was used to create mosaics. This art form uses small, decorative ceramic squares to form a design or picture. Today tile is a popular building material because it is long-lasting, unaffected by water, and easily cleaned. It is used in shopping centers, tunnels, lobbies, and bathrooms.

Subjects to Study

General mathematics, mechanical drawing, shop courses, blueprint reading, art courses, physical education

Discover More

Try making a mosaic. Check a craft or tile store for materials and directions.

Related Jobs

Bricklayers, concrete masons, marblesetters, plasterers, stonemasons, terrazzo workers

Earnings	Education and Training	Job Outlook
Low	High school/Specialized training	Little change

Production Occupations

Precision Assemblers

Job Description

Precision assemblers are highly experienced and trained workers who put together complicated products such as computers, appliances, and electronic equipment. Their work is detailed and must be done accurately. They follow directions from engineers and use a variety of tools and precise measuring instruments.

Working Conditions

The conditions under which precision assemblers work depend on their type of job. Electronics assemblers work at tables in clean, well-lighted, dust-free rooms. Aircraft or manufacturing assemblers work around grease, oil, and noise. They may have to lift and fit heavy objects. Precision assemblers' work schedules vary with the shift schedule of their workplace.

Subjects to Study

Mathematics, science, computer education, shop courses, electronics

Discover More

Get a kit and try to assemble a radio or some other electronic equipment.

Related Jobs

Welders, ophthalmic laboratory technicians, machine operators

Earnings	Education and Training	Job Outlook

Very low	High school/Specialized training	Decreasing

Blue-Collar Worker Supervisors

Job Description

Blue-collar worker supervisors are in charge of groups of workers. They create work schedules, monitor workers, check machinery, and train new workers. They are often in charge of expensive equipment or systems. A supervisor's main responsibility is making sure that work gets done.

Working Conditions

Supervisors may work in a shop or outdoors. They are on the job before other workers arrive and stay after others leave. They may work shifts and holidays or weekends. Some work on a rotating shift, while others always work the same shift.

Something Extra

In today's work world, being a supervisor means more than being the boss. Employees' opinions in making decisions are becoming increasingly important. A supervisor acts more as a helper in guiding the group and as a communicator between employees and management.

Subjects to Study

Mathematics, English, communication skills, speech

Discover More

Communicating is an important part of this job. How well do you communicate? Learn to talk to others as well as listen.

Related Jobs

Retail store or department managers, sales managers, clerical supervisors, bank officers, head tellers, hotel managers, postmasters, head cooks, head nurses, surveyors

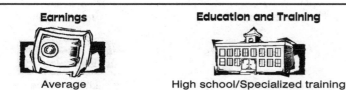

Earnings	Education and Training	Job Outlook
Average	High school/Specialized training	Decreasing

Butchers and Meat, Poultry, and Fish Cutters

Something Extra

In the 1800s, a Swiss naturalist connected two facts. One, the brain contains phosphorus; and, two, phosphorus is found in fish. Therefore, he decided that eating fish helped develop the brain. Actually phosphorus is found in most foods, so eating fish before a test isn't a guarantee of passing your classes or getting As.

Job Description

Butchers and meat, poultry, and fish cutters cut animal meat into small pieces to be sold to consumers. They remove bones from certain cuts of meat and inedible parts such as the head, tail, and scales of fish. They package and display meat, fish, and poultry for customers.

Working Conditions

Butchers and meatcutters may work behind the meat counter in a small market or in large refrigerated rooms on an assembly line. Work areas must be clean and sanitary, although they are often cold and damp. These workers have the highest rate of work-related injuries and illnesses of any industry.

Subjects to Study

English, communication skills, mathematics, home economics, food preparation

Discover More

Learn about the different cuts of meat, fish, and poultry available. Visit the meat department of a grocery store to see the different cuts and talk to a butcher there.

Related Jobs

Bakers, chefs, cooks, food preparation workers

Earnings	Education and Training	Job Outlook

Low	Specialized training	Little change

Inpectors, Testers, and Graders

Job Description

Inspectors, testers, and graders examine products before releasing them to consumers by looking at, listening to, or feeling the products, or by tasting or smelling them. Products must meet certain quality standards. Inspectors may reject the product, send it back to be fixed, or fix the problem themselves. If the product checks out, it is marked as passing the inspection.

Something Extra

Inspectors do not test every single item that comes off the assembly line. Car manufacturers may have a certain number of cars that are tested—for example, every eighth car. Increasingly, inspection is occurring on the line during the production process rather than just on the final product. Problems or defects can be detected earlier this way.

Working Conditions

Working conditions may be noisy and dirty or quiet and clean, depending on the industry. Some inspectors move from place to place, while others have a work station. Some sit, while others stand all day. Some inspect the same item, while others have a variety of items to examine. Lifting is sometimes necessary. Working evenings, nights, and weekends is possible.

Subjects to Study

English, mathematics, shop courses, blueprint reading, mechanics

Discover More

Learn how to contact a company if you are not satisfied with its product. Check the packaging of some products in your home for a consumer telephone number or an address.

Related Jobs

Construction and building inspectors, compliance officers except construction

Earnings	Education and Training	Job Outlook
Low	High school/Specialized training	Decreasing

Boilermakers

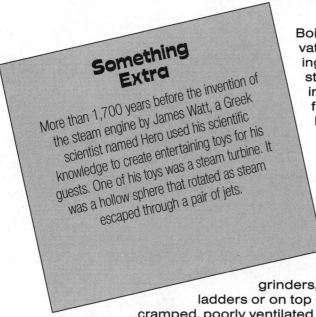

Something Extra

More than 1,700 years before the invention of the steam engine by James Watt, a Greek scientist named Hero used his scientific knowledge to create entertaining toys for his guests. One of his toys was a steam turbine. It was a hollow sphere that rotated as steam escaped through a pair of jets.

Job Description

Boilermakers build and assemble boilers, vats, and other large tanks used for storing liquids and gases. Boilers supply steam for electric turbines and for heating and power systems in buildings, factories, and ships. Because most boilers last for 35 years or more, repairing and maintaining them is another part of a boilermaker's work.

Working Conditions

Boilermakers work 40-hour weeks with occasional overtime to meet deadlines. They often use potentially dangerous equipment such as acetylene torches and power grinders, handle heavy parts, and work on ladders or on top of large vessels. Work may be done in cramped, poorly ventilated vats and boilers. To avoid injury, they may wear safety glasses and shoes, hardhats, and protective clothing.

Subjects to Study

Mathematics, shop courses, blueprint reading, welding, machine metalworking

Discover More

Most boilermakers belong to labor unions. Learn more about labor unions. Find out what labor unions are active in your community.

Related Jobs

Assemblers, blacksmiths, instrument makers, ironworkers, machinists, millwrights, patternmakers, plumbers, sheet-metal workers, tool and die makers, welders

Earnings	Education and Training	Job Outlook
Average	High school/Specialized training	Decreasing

Jewelers

Job Description

Jewelers use precious metals and stones such as gold and diamonds to make necklaces, rings, bracelets, and other jewelry. They may specialize in one or more areas of the jewelry field—buying, design, gem cutting, repair, sales, or appraisal. This work requires a high degree of skill and attention to detail.

Working Conditions

Jewelers do most of their work seated in comfortable surroundings. They must be careful using chemicals, sawing and drilling tools, and torches. Their work is delicate and detailed. Because the materials they work with are quite valuable, strict security measures must be observed. They normally work 40 to 48 hours a week, including evenings and Saturdays.

Something Extra

The Hope Diamond is kept in the Smithsonian Institution in Washington, D.C. More than 20 deaths have been blamed on this jewel, which is supposedly cursed. Through the centuries its owners have been killed by wild dogs, beheaded, and met other tragic misfortunes. Some people believe that the last owner escaped death by giving it to the museum.

Subjects to Study

Mathematics, art, mechanical drawing, chemistry, computer skills, blueprint reading

Discover More

Making jewelry can be an interesting and even profitable hobby. Find out if your school's art department offers a jewelry making class.

Related Jobs

Polishers, dental laboratory technicians, gem cutters, hand engravers, watch makers, repairers

Earnings	Education and Training	Job Outlook

Low-average	High school/Specialized training	Little change

Machinists and Tool Programmers

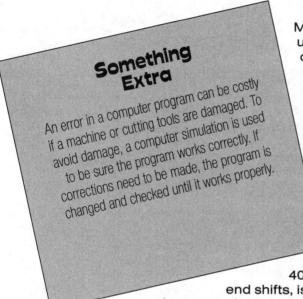

Something Extra

An error in a computer program can be costly if a machine or cutting tools are damaged. To avoid damage, a computer simulation is used to be sure the program works correctly. If corrections need to be made, the program is changed and checked until it works properly.

Job Description

Machinists produce precise metal parts using lathes, drill presses, and milling machines. They often make specialized parts or one-of-a-kind items. Tool programmers specialize in computer programming to make parts. A computer gives instructions to a machine that follows each step until the part is completed.

Working Conditions

Machinists, working in well-lighted and ventilated workshops, wear safety glasses and earplugs for protection from high-speed machine tools. Tool programmers may work in offices near the machine shop. A 40-hour week, including evening and weekend shifts, is common, with overtime hours during heavy production periods.

Subjects to Study

Mathematics, shop courses, blueprint reading, metalworking, drafting, physics, mechanical drawing, computer skills, electronics

Discover More

Visit a machine shop in your community. The high school shop or a vocational school are some places where you can find metalworking machines.

Related Jobs

Tool and die makers, tool and die designers, tool planners, instrument makers, blacksmiths, gunsmiths, locksmiths, metal patternmakers, welders

Earnings	Education and Training	Job Outlook

Average	High school/Specialized training	Decreasing

Metalworking and Plastics-Working Machine Operators

Job Description

Many products are made of metal and plastic parts. The workers who produce these parts can be separated into two groups: those who set up the machines and those who tend the machines during production. These machines cut and form all types of metal and plastic parts.

Working Conditions

Metalworking and plastics-working machine operators work 40-hour weeks in clean, well-lighted work areas. Overtime, evening, and weekend work is common. These workers operate powerful, high speed machines that can be dangerous. Safety glasses and earplugs are used for protection.

Something Extra

To make plastic two-liter bottles, such as the kind soft drinks are sold in, a technique called blow-molding is used. The blow-molding machine forces hot air into a mold that contains a plastic tube. As the air moves into the mold, the plastic tube is inflated to the shape of the mold and the bottle is formed.

Subjects to Study

Mathematics, English, shop courses, blueprint reading

Discover More

Think about the items you use daily, such as pens, telephones, and radios. Most were produced by metalworking and plastics-working machine operators. Make a list of other items made by these workers.

Related Jobs

Machinists, tool and die makers, extruding and forming machine operators, woodworking machine operators, metal patternmakers

Earnings	Education and Training	Job Outlook

Low	High school/Specialized training	Decreasing

Tool and Die Makers

Job Description

Tool and die makers are highly skilled workers. Toolmakers create precision tools that cut, shape, and form metal and other materials. Diemakers construct dies, which are metal forms used to shape metal in stamping and forging machines. Tool and die makers must have a broader knowledge of machining operations, mathematics, and blueprint reading than most other machining workers.

Something Extra

Computer aided design (CAD) is often used to make new parts. The computer program can be used to design tools and dies. When the design is ready, it is sent to a computer-controlled machine which makes the tool or die. These programs can be saved and used to make parts in the future.

Working Conditions

Tool and die makers work in toolrooms around machinery. These workers must follow safety rules and wear protective equipment such as safety glasses and earplugs. Standing and lifting are part of this job. Most work day shifts, although overtime and Saturday work are common.

Subjects to Study

Mathematics, shop courses, blueprint reading, metalworking, drafting, machine shop, mechanical drawing

Discover More

Test your patience. Get an old machine that isn't wanted anymore. Take it apart and look at the different parts. Try putting it back together.

Related Jobs

Machinists, moldmakers, instrument makers, metalmaking machine operators, tool programmers, blacksmiths, gunsmiths, locksmiths, metal patternmakers, welders

Earnings	Education and Training	Job Outlook

Average	Specialized training/Associate	Decreasing

Welders, Cutters, and Welding Machine Operators

Job Description

Welders apply heat to metal parts to permanently join them. Because of its strength, welding is used on parts of ships, automobiles, spacecraft, and thousands of other products. Welders may do the welding by hand or machine. Welding machine operators make sure that welding machines operate correctly. Cutters use heat to cut and dismantle metal objects.

Working Conditions

Welders and cutters are frequently exposed to potential hazards and wear protective gear to prevent burns and protect them from eye injuries and falling objects. Ventilation at the workplace must meet strict guidelines to protect workers from dangerous fumes. In some work settings, few hazards or discomforts are encountered by workers.

Something Extra

The welding torch is usually associated with building bridges, ships, and automobiles, but it also can be an artist's tool. Sculptors often use metal in their art and use a welding torch to connect the parts. Welding was used on the gigantic Statue of Liberty, which is made of an iron framework covered with sheets of copper.

Subjects to Study

Shop courses, blueprint reading, shop mathematics, mechanical drawing, physics, chemistry, metallurgy

Discover More

To learn more about this occupation, write to: American Welding Society, 550 NW LeJeune Rd., Miami, FL 33126-5699.

Related Jobs

Blacksmiths, forge shop workers, all-round machinists, machine-tool operators, tool and die makers, millwrights, sheet-metal workers, boilermakers, metal sculptors, lathe and turning, milling and planing, punching and stamping press, and rolling machine operators

Earnings	Education and Training	Job Outlook
Low	High school/Specialized training	Little change

Electric Power Generating Plant Operators and Power Distributors and Dispatchers

Something Extra

The weather forecast is useful to power plant dispatchers for planning electrical needs. During the summer, a long period of extreme heat will cause air-conditioning needs to rise. More electricity will be needed. In the winter, severe blizzards or storms may cause power lines to fail. Workers need to prepare for emergency repairs.

Job Description

Electric power generating plant operators control the machinery that generates electricity. They start or stop generators as power requirements change. Power distributors and dispatchers make sure that users are receiving enough electricity. They plan for times when more electricity is needed and handle emergencies.

Working Conditions

Because electricity is used 24 hours a day, operators, dispatchers, and distributors often work nights and weekends on rotating shifts. Work on rotating shifts can be stressful and tiring because of the constant change in living and sleep patterns. This work is not physically demanding, but requires constant attention to the controls.

Subjects to Study

Mathematics, science, English

Discover More

Talk to the public relations department of the local electric company. Find out where your electricity is generated.

Related Jobs

Stationary engineers, water and sewage treatment plant operators, waterworks pump-station operators, chemical operators, refinery operators

Earnings	Education and Training	Job Outlook

High	High school/Specialized training	Decreasing

Stationary Engineers

Job Description

Stationary engineers operate and maintain equipment which provides air-conditioning, heat, and ventilation to large buildings. In industry, the equipment may supply electricity, steam, or other types of power. The word "stationary" indicates that these engines are similar to those on a train or ship; however, the engines are not in vehicles that move.

Working Conditions

Stationary engineers work 5-day, 40-hour weeks. Holiday and weekend work is often required. Although their work area is clean, these workers are exposed to heat, dust, dirt, and noise from equipment. They may crawl or kneel when working on equipment. Hazards of this job include burns, electric shock, and injury from moving parts.

Something Extra

The Sears Tower in Chicago, one of the world's tallest buildings, provides offices for 16,500 workers in 110 stories. Its temperature is controlled by 17,000 tons of refrigeration equipment, but the building will soon have its own power station. An underground electricity substation is planned to supply power for the building and surrounding city center.

Subjects to Study

Mathematics, computer skills, mechanical drawing, machine-shop practice, chemistry, physical education

Discover More

Learn how to maintain and care for machines in your home such as the lawnmower and electric tools. Learn what tools to use, how to lubricate the machines, and how to keep them in good repair.

Related Jobs

Nuclear reactor operators, power station operators, water and wastewater treatment plant operators, waterworks pump-station operators, chemical operators, refinery operators

Earnings	Education and Training	Job Outlook
Average	High school/Specialized training	Decreasing

Water and Wastewater Treatment Plant Operators

Something Extra

Maintaining a water supply was a problem when Louis XIV was king of France. He demanded that water be supplied for 1,400 fountains at his palace at Versailles. The amount of water needed was nearly as much as the whole city of Paris required. If the king took a stroll through the garden and the fountains were not working, the overseer was fined.

Job Description

Water treatment plant operators treat water so that it is safe to drink. Wastewater plant operators remove harmful pollution from wastewater. These workers also read and interpret meters and gauges and adjust controls. They take water samples, perform water analyses, and test and adjust chemicals in the water, such as chorine.

Working Conditions

Water and wastewater treatment plant operators work both indoors and outdoors and may be exposed to noise, odors, and dangerous gases. Because the plants operate 24 hours a day, operators work one of three 8-hour shifts and rotate working on weekends and holidays. They work overtime during emergencies.

Subjects to Study

Mathematics, chemistry, biology

Discover More

Find out where your local water supply is located. Visit a water or wastewater treatment plant.

Related Jobs

Boiler operators, gas-compressor operators, power plant operators, power reactor operators, stationary engineers, turbine operators, chemical plant operators, petroleum refinery operators

Earnings	Education and Training	Job Outlook

Average	Specialized training/Associate	Little change

Prepress Workers

Job Description

Prepress workers prepare materials for printing presses. They perform a variety of tasks such as typesetting, designing page layout, taking photographs, and making printing plates. Through the use of personal computers, customers often show workers how they want their printed material to look. Prepress workers have different titles depending on their jobs.

Working Conditions

Prepress workers work in clean, air-conditioned areas with little noise. They may experience eyestrain and backaches from working at video monitors, and some work with harmful chemicals. Most work 8-hour days. Those working for newspapers may work night shifts, weekends, and holidays. Meeting deadlines can be stressful.

Something Extra

Desktop publishing has changed the printing industry. Many customers now use computers to design material that looks like the finished product. The printer then gets a computer disk with the customer's preset design. The printer often uses complete digital imaging, which converts material on the disk directly onto a printing plate, eliminating many of printers' previous layout and design duties.

Subjects to Study

Mathematics, English, communication skills, writing skills, electronics, computer skills, art courses

Discover More

Learn how to use word processing and graphic software packages on a computer. Design your own greeting cards to celebrate special occasions.

Related Jobs

Sign painters, jewelers, decorators, engravers, graphic artists, clerk typists, computer terminal system operators, keypunch operators, telegraphic-typewriter operators

Earnings	Education and Training	Job Outlook

Average	High school/Specialized training	Decreasing

Printing Press Operators

Job Description

Printing press operators prepare, operate, and maintain the printing presses in a pressroom. They check the paper and ink, make sure the paper feeders are stocked, and monitor the presses as they are running. Computerized presses allow press operators to make adjustments at a control panel by pressing buttons.

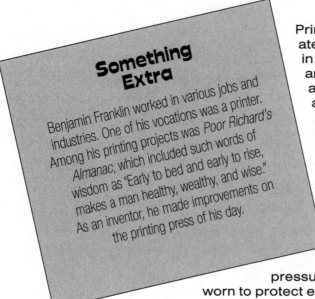

Something Extra

Benjamin Franklin worked in various jobs and industries. One of his vocations was a printer. Among his printing projects was *Poor Richard's Almanac*, which included such words of wisdom as "Early to bed and early to rise, makes a man healthy, wealthy, and wise." As an inventor, he made improvements on the printing press of his day.

Working Conditions

Printing press operators are on their feet most of the time. Their work can be physically and mentally demanding and sometimes tedious. Often, they are under pressure to meet deadlines. Earplugs are worn to protect ears from noisy machinery. Many work evening, night, and overtime shifts.

Subjects to Study

Mathematics, English, communication skills, writing skills, computer skills, chemistry, electronics, physics

Discover More

Visit a newspaper or printing company. Observe the different types of presses and how they are operated. Talk to a press operator.

Related Jobs

Papermaking machine operators, shoemaking machine operators, bindery machine operators, precision machine operators

Earnings	Education and Training	Job Outlook

Low	Specialized training	Little change

Bindery Workers

Job Description

Bindery workers operate and maintain machines that "bind" the pages of books, magazines, pamphlets, and other reading materials. To bind reading material, machines fold, cut, gather, glue, stitch, sew, trim, and wrap pages to form a product. These workers' job duties depend on the kind of material being bound.

Working Conditions

Binding jobs can be physically demanding, requiring lifting, standing, kneeling, and carrying. Workers often work on an assembly line, so tasks may be boring and repetitive. Most work a standard 40-hour week. A small number of bookbinders work in hand binderies, designing special bindings for limited editions or restoring rare books.

Something Extra

The cover tears, the pages start to fade, and the book comes apart. Rare books that are hundreds and even thousands of years old are restored by bookbinders. Bookbinders must work carefully with special tools and chemicals to save these priceless treasures. The binding is done by hand, which requires a lot of knowledge about materials and the history of binding.

Subjects to Study

Mathematics, English, art courses, shop courses

Discover More

Find some old books in your home or at garage sales that are coming apart. Try repairing them.

Related Jobs

Papermaking machine operators, press workers, precision machine operators

Earnings	Education and Training	Job Outlook

Very low	High school/Specialized training	Little change

Apparel Workers

Job Description

Apparel workers transform cloth, leather, and fur into clothing and other products. Many also care for and clean these products and do alterations. First a pattern is created, then the fabric is spread and cut. The material is then sewn together, usually by a machine. A custom tailor makes the entire garment based on a customer's measurements.

Working Conditions

Working conditions for apparel workers vary by organization and type of job. Older factories are usually congested and poorly lit and poorly ventilated, while newer factories tend to be more comfortable and well-lit. Laundries and dry cleaners are hot and noisy, while retail stores are quiet. Most work a 40-hour week, including some evenings or weekends.

Subjects to Study

Mathematics, home economics courses, sewing, English, computer skills

Discover More

Get a pattern for a simple project made from cloth. Follow the pattern direction to make the project.

Related Jobs

Metalworking and plastics-working machine operators, textile machine operators, shoe sewing machine operators, precision woodworkers, precision assemblers, shoe and leather workers, upholsterers, tool and die makers, precision welders

Earnings	Education and Training	Job Outlook

Very low	Specialized training	Decreasing

Shoe and Leather Workers and Repairers

Job Description

Shoe and leather workers cut leather using patterns. Then they put the pieces together to make products such as shoes, horse saddles, and luggage. Repairers extend the life of worn leather goods by attaching new parts, such as heels and soles on shoes, or resewing seams or replacing handles and linings in suitcases and handbags.

Working Conditions

Workers in factories usually work a 40-hour week. Their work areas can be noisy, and odors from leather and dyes are often present. Workers in repair shops may work nights and weekends. Self-employed repairers usually work overtime.

Something Extra

Before shoemaking machinery was used, shoemakers—called journeymen—traveled from home to home hawking their skills. The journeyman would use the family's leather to make a year's supply of shoes for the entire family. This method of making shoes was known as "whipping the cat."

Subjects to Study

Mathematics, shop courses, sewing courses, art courses, business courses

Discover More

Learn more about working with leather. Try a project using a leather working kit.

Related Jobs

Dressmakers, designers, patternmakers, furriers

Earnings	Education and Training	Job Outlook

Low	Specialized training	Decreasing

Textile Machinery Operators

Job Description

Textile machinery operators care for and operate the machines used to produce textile goods used in all types of products, from clothing to materials in tires. They oversee many machines that prepare fibers for spinning, make yarn, and produce fabric. They make sure machines are supplied with yarn, repair breaks in yarn, and make machine repairs when needed.

Working Conditions

Textile machinery operators usually work 40 hours each week. Rotating schedules are used for night and weekend shifts. Protective glasses, masks, shoes, and clothing may be needed. Operators stand during most of their shifts.

Subjects to Study

Mathematics, English, shop courses, computer skills

Discover More

Some fabrics are made from natural fibers while others are made from manmade fibers. Learn about different types of fabrics by visiting a fabric shop.

Related Jobs

Extruding and forming machine operators and tenders, textile bleaching and dyeing machine operators, metal fabrication and plastics manufacturing setters and setup operators

Earnings	Education and Training	Job Outlook

Very low	High school/Specialized training	Decreasing

Upholsterers

Job Description

Upholsterers are skilled craft workers who make new furniture or repair or recondition old furniture. They may pick up and deliver furniture or help customers select new furniture coverings. Ordering supplies and equipment and keeping business records are also duties of this occupation.

Working Conditions

Upholsterers may work in comfortable shops or factories, but some work in small and dusty areas. These workers stand most of the day and do a lot of bending and heavy lifting. Working in awkward positions for short periods of time is sometimes required.

Something Extra

Skilled craft workers often use tools especially developed for their trade. Upholsterers work with common hand tools such as staple guns, staple removers, pliers, shears, and sewing machines. Special tools such as webbing stretchers pull the material used to hold the springs in place. Needles that are round or very thick and large are used to sew hard-to-reach places.

Subjects to Study

Mathematics, home economics courses, sewing, upholstery, shop courses, woodworking, art courses

Discover More

To learn more about this occupation, talk to an upholsterer or write: Upholstery and Allied Industries Division, United Steelworkers of America, Local 18, 5320 W. North Avenue, Chicago, IL 60639.

Related Jobs

Fur cutters, furniture finishers, pattern and model makers, webbing tackers, casket coverers

Earnings	Education and Training	Job Outlook

Very low	Specialized training	Decreasing

Woodworkers

Job Description

Woodworkers make needed products from wood and are employed at many stages of the process during which lumber is transformed into finished products. They operate machines that cut, shape, assemble, and finish wood to make doors, cabinets, paneling, furniture, and many other products. Precision woodworkers make rare or customized items, which requires great skill.

Working Conditions

Working conditions of woodworkers vary from industry to industry and from job to job. But most of these workers handle heavy materials, stand for long periods of time, and risk exposure to dust and air pollutants. Workers may wear ear plugs, eye goggles, dust or vapor masks, and protective clothing.

Subjects to Study

Mathematics, science, computer skills, shop courses, woodworking, blueprint reading, mechanics

Discover More

Ask an adult to help you with a woodworking project such as building a shelf or making a wooden toy.

Related Jobs

Precision metalworkers, metalworking and plastics-working machine operators, metal fabricators, molders and shapers, leather workers

Earnings	Education and Training	Job Outlook

Very low	High school/Specialized training	Decreasing

Dental Laboratory Technicians

Job Description

Dental laboratory technicians fill the prescribed orders of dentists. Dentists send directions and molds of patients' mouths to the technicians' laboratories. They use these to make dentures (false teeth), crowns, and bridges to be placed in patients' mouths. In some laboratories, technicians perform all stages of the work, while in others, each does only a few.

Working Conditions

Dental laboratory technicians usually have their own workbenches in clean, well-lighted areas. Their work is very delicate and takes a lot of time. Salaried technicians usually work 40 hours a week, but self-employed technicians often work longer hours.

Something Extra

Tooth decay has been a problem for many centuries, and even kings and queens have suffered tooth loss. When Elizabeth I was queen of England (1558-1603), she lost her front teeth. To make her face appear fuller, she put pieces of cloth under her lips. Other members of the royal court had ornamental teeth made from silver or gold.

Subjects to Study

Sciences, art, metal and wood shop, drafting, business courses, management courses

Discover More

Talk to a friend who wears or has worn braces. Find out what the orthodontist did before your friend's braces were made.

Related Jobs

Arch-support technicians, orthotics technicians (braces and surgical supports), prosthetics technicians (artificial limbs and appliances), opticians, ophthalmic laboratory technicians

Earnings	Education and Training	Job Outlook

Average	Specialized training/Associate	Little change

Ophthalmic Laboratory Technicians

Something Extra

Eyeglasses were once thought unattractive, but today designer eyeglass frames are often worn to make a fashion statement. Even people who do not need to wear glasses to correct vision problems, sometimes do. With so many different styles and colors, some people buy two or three pairs instead of only one.

Job Description

Ophthalmic laboratory technicians make lenses for prescription glasses. Some make lenses for other optical instruments, such as telescopes and binoculars. They read the prescribed directions from eye doctors and mark the lenses to know where to grind the curves. Then they polish the lenses to remove the rough edges and put them in frames for the patient.

Working Conditions

Ophthalmic laboratory technicians work in clean, quiet laboratories without much public contact. They wear goggles to protect their eyes and spend much of their time standing. A 5-day, 40-hour week is normal. Some work part-time.

Subjects to Study

Mathematics, science courses, English

Discover More

You may be able to observe an ophthalmic laboratory at a large optical store in your community. Sometimes the laboratory is a windowed area in the store where you can watch from a distance.

Related Jobs

Biomedical equipment technicians, dental laboratory technicians, orthodontic technicians, prosthetics technicians, instrument repairers

Earnings	Education and Training	Job Outlook

Very low	High school/Specialized training	Little change

Painting and Coating Machine Operators

Job Description

Painting and coating machine operators cover everything from cars to candy with paints, plastics, varnishes, chocolates, or special coating solutions. The most common method of applying paints and coatings is by spraying the article with a solution. Coating is done to make a product look more appealing to a customer or to protect materials from deteriorating.

Working Conditions

Painting and coating machine operators work indoors and may be exposed to dangerous fumes. They wear masks or respirators that cover their noses and mouth, to protect themselves from these fumes. They stand, bend, and crouch in uncomfortable positions to reach all parts of a product. Most work 40-hour weeks, but self-employed automotive painters often work more.

Something Extra

Workers in this occupation handle diverse products. Paper coating operators use spray painters to put "size"—the finish—on paper. Silvering applicators spray glass with solutions of silver, copper, and tin to make mirrors. Enrobing machine operators coat bakery goods with melted chocolate, cheese, oils, and sugar. Automotive painters use spray guns to apply coats of paint to automobiles.

Subjects to Study

Shop courses, art courses

Discover More

An auto body repair shop is a place to observe spray painting in action. Try to find one that will let you watch, although you will probably have to observe from a distance because of the fumes.

Related Jobs

Construction and maintenance painters, electrolytic metal platers, hand painting, coating and decorating occupations

Earnings	Education and Training	Job Outlook
Very low	Specialized training	Little change

Photographic Process Workers

Something Extra

Adapting to new technology is essential in photoprocessing. In recent years, computers have been used more than darkrooms to develop and alter film much more rapidly than in the past. One-hour photoprocessing stores are popular with customers who want to see their photos quickly. More changes in photoprocessing are expected in the future.

Job Description

Photographic process workers help photographers by developing film, making prints and slides, and enlarging and re-touching photographs. They also restore damaged and faded photographs. Most of these workers operate various machines to complete their tasks.

Working Conditions

Photographic process workers work in clean, comfortable offices, photo-finishing laboratories, and one-hour minilabs. Their work is repetitious and must be done rapidly and accurately. They are exposed to chemicals and wear gloves and aprons for protection. Forty-hour weeks are normal, including some weekend and overtime work.

Subjects to Study

Mathematics, art, computer science, photography

Discover More

Does your school have a darkroom? If so, find out who develops the photographs for the school newspaper and yearbook and watch them doing their work.

Related Jobs

Chemical laboratory technicians, crime laboratory analysts, food testers, medical laboratory assistants, metallurgical technicians, quality control technicians, engravers, photolithographers

Earnings	Education and Training	Job Outlook

Very low	High school/Specialized training	Little change

Transportation and Material Moving Occupations

Bus Drivers

Job Description

Bus drivers transport people from place to place following a time schedule and specific route. Intercity bus drivers transport people long distances within a state or throughout the country. Local transit bus drivers travel in a particular city or county. School bus drivers drive students to and from school and school-related events.

Working Conditions

Bus drivers deal with heavy traffic and many passengers, often in bad weather. Some work nights, weekends, and holidays; others travel overnight away from their homes. A five-day work week including Saturdays and Sundays is common. Intercity bus travel tends to be seasonal, and junior drivers may work infrequently during the winter. School bus drivers, who account for three of every four bus drivers, work part-time.

Subjects to Study

English, communication skills, mathematics, driver's training, first aid

Discover More

Take a ride on a commercial bus and talk to the bus driver about this occupation. Observe what the bus driver does to communicate with passengers and care for the bus.

Related Jobs

Taxi drivers, truck drivers, chauffeurs

Earnings	Education and Training	Job Outlook

Low	High school	Little change

Material Moving Equipment Operators

Job Description

Material moving equipment operators load and unload trucks and ships using equipment such as cranes, bulldozers, and forklifts. They move construction materials, logs, coal, and other heavy materials short distances around factories, warehouses, and construction sites. They sometimes set up, clean, and repair equipment.

Working Conditions

Most material moving equipment operators work outside in all types of weather. Others work inside in warehouses or factories. Some machines, such as bulldozers, are noisy and may shake the driver. Safety measures are taken to avoid accidents.

Something Extra

Learning how to operate moving equipment to perform a particular job is not easy. An operator must position the machinery in the correct place to complete the task. This is done by moving levers or foot pedals, pushing buttons, or moving dials. The machine must be moved carefully and correctly to avoid tipping.

Subjects to Study

Shop classes, auto mechanics, driver's education

Discover More

Look for material moving machines in your community. What do they move? In what businesses are they used? How are the operators controlling the machines?

Related Jobs

Truck drivers, bus drivers, manufacturing equipment operators, farmers

Earnings	Education and Training	Job Outlook

Low	High school/Specialized training	Little change

Rail Transportation Workers

Job Description

Rail transportation workers include railroad employees as well as subway and streetcar operators. Railroad engineers operate locomotives that transport passengers and cargo. Conductors are responsible for the cargo and passengers. They work with brake operators to ensure that cars are added or removed from the train correctly. Brakemen do physical work such as removing the cars and throwing track switches to allow trains to change tracks.

Something Extra

In the late 1800s, wealthy citizens sometimes owned private railroad cars. Some cars even included luxury items such as sunken bathtubs, barbers' chairs, and pipe organs. The cars were usually decorated with very expensive materials. Rather than owning a railroad car, some wealthy people rented one when traveling.

Working Conditions

Railroads operate 24 hours a day, 7 days a week. Their employees must work nights, weekends, and holidays. Freight train workers have no set schedule, but are called to work when it is their turn—often on short notice. Railroad workers may spend several nights a week away from home. Some work outside and do physically demanding work.

Subjects to Study

Mathematics, mechanics, driver's education, physical education

Discover More

Visit a railroad station or ride a train and observe the different workers.

Related Jobs

Truck drivers, taxi drivers, bus drivers

Earnings	Education and Training	Job Outlook

Average	High school/Specialized training	Little change

Taxi Drivers and Chauffeurs

Job Description

Taxi drivers and chauffeurs pick up and drive people to their destinations in cars, limousines, or vans. Taxi drivers charge passengers a fare when destinations are reached, such as airports, hotels, or restaurants. Chauffeurs pamper their passengers by providing extras such as newspapers, drinks, music, and television.

Working Conditions

Taxi drivers and chauffeurs often have to load and unload heavy luggage and packages. Dealing with bad weather, heavy traffic, and rude customers is part of this job, and drivers must be alert at all times. Taxi drivers may work at all times of the day or night, seven days a week. Chauffeurs' work is often dictated by their customers' or employers' needs.

Something Extra

Chauffeur is a French word meaing "stoker." In the past, when cars were driven by steam, hired drivers kept the cars moving by keeping the boiler fire going. This was done by "stoking" the fire. The French word *chauffeur* remains in use today, even though steam-powered cars are no longer used.

Subjects to Study

English, mathematics, physical education, driver's education

Discover More

Take a taxi ride and talk to the driver about this occupation.

Related Jobs

Ambulance drivers, bus drivers, truck drivers

Earnings	Education and Training	Job Outlook
Very low	Specialized training	Little change

Truck Drivers

Something Extra

Long-distance trucking runs may last for several days or even weeks. Stops are made only for gas, food, and loading and unloading. On such long runs, two drivers may work together. One driver sleeps in a berth built into the truck while the other drives. This type of truck run is called a 'sleeper.'

Job Description

Truck drivers move and deliver goods between factories, terminals, warehouses, stores, and homes. They maintain their trucks, check for fuel and oil, ensure that brakes and lights are in working order, and make minor repairs. They also load and unload the goods they transport.

Working Conditions

Driving in poor weather, heavy traffic, and mountains can be stressful. Local drivers normally work 48 or more hours each week. Although most have regular routes, some drive different routes each day. Some self-employed long-distance drivers spend 240 days on the road each year. Long runs can be boring, lonely, and tiring.

Subjects to Study

Mathematics, driver's education, physical education, communication skills, accounting, business

Discover More

Talk to a local or long-distance truck driver. Ask what is good and bad about this occupation.

Related Jobs

Ambulance drivers, bus drivers, chauffeurs, taxi drivers

Earnings	Education and Training	Job Outlook

Low	High school/Specialized training	Little change

Water Transportation Workers

Job Description

Workers in water transportation use all types of water vehicles on oceans, the Great Lakes, rivers, canals, and other waterways. Captains or masters are in charge of a vessel and the crew. Deck officers or mates assist the captain. Seamen or deckhands perform work such as maintenance, steering, and loading and unloading cargo. Pilots guide ships through harbors and narrow waterways.

Something Extra

Merchant mariners on Great Lakes ships normally work for 60 consecutive days, then have 30 days off. Living for long periods of time on a ship is a very hard. Also, little job security exists because a mariner is hired for one voyage at a time. During the winter when the lakes are frozen there is no work.

Working Conditions

Workers in water transportation must cope with all types of weather. Some work 8- or 12-hour shifts and go home each night. Others spend long periods of time away from home. They face injury or even death from falling overboard and working with heavy machinery or dangerous cargo.

Subjects to Study

Mathematics, physical education, swimming, first aid

Discover More

Learn about some of the great ships and shipwrecks, such as the sinking of the *Titanic*, during the early part of the 1900s.

Related Jobs

Fishing vessel captains, ferryboat operators, hatchtenders

Earnings	Education and Training	Job Outlook
Very low-high	High school/Bachelor's	Decreasing

Handlers, Equipment Cleaners, Helpers, and Laborers

Something Extra

Automation of repetitious work affects the employment growth of laborers. For example, self-service gasoline pumps mean that service station attendants are no longer needed to fill gas tanks. Similarly, workers in carwashes may no longer be needed because automatic carwashes do their jobs.

Job Description

Handlers, equipment cleaners, helpers, and laborers perform a variety of entry-level tasks from moving boxes to cleaning work areas. They follow the directions of a supervisor and have little chance to make any type of decision. They do routine tasks that allow skilled or experienced workers to work more smoothly.

Working Conditions

Most laborers do physically demanding work involving lifting, kneeling, and crawling. Some work at great heights or outdoors. Some are exposed to harmful chemicals or loud or dangerous machinery and may wear safety clothing. Some work late at night, while others work very early in the morning.

Subjects to Study

Reading, basic mathematics, physical education

Discover More

Make a list of industries and the jobs that laborers and helpers do in those industries. What laborers do you see in your community?

Related Jobs

Roustabouts, loggers, groundskeepers, machine operators, construction craft workers, assemblers, mechanics, repairers

Earnings	Education and Training	Job Outlook

Very low	High school	Little change

Job Opportunities in the Armed Forces

Armed Forces

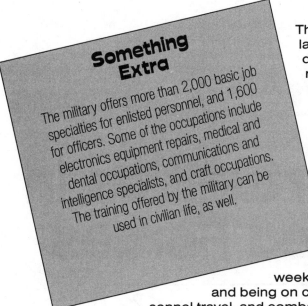

Something Extra

The military offers more than 2,000 basic job specialties for enlisted personnel, and 1,600 for officers. Some of the occupations include electronics equipment repairs, medical and dental occupations, communications and intelligence specialists, and craft occupations. The training offered by the military can be used in civilian life, as well.

Job Description

The Armed Forces are the United States' largest employer. Maintaining a strong defense requires many activities, such as running hospitals, repairing helicopters, programming computers, and operating nuclear reactors. Military jobs range from clerical work to professional positions to construction work.

Working Conditions

People who sign an enlistment contract are legally bound to serve in the Armed Forces for a specified time period, and life in the military is very disciplined. Rules govern life. Normal eight-hour days and five-day weeks are usual. Working weekends or nights and being on call may be required. Many military personnel travel, and combat is always a possibility.

Subjects to Study

Mathematics, English, business, sciences

Discover More

Would you enjoy military life? Talk to people who have served in the Armed Forces. Contact a recruiter to find out about a particular branch of the military. (Remember, though, that a recruiter's job is to get people to join).

Related Jobs

Nearly any civilian job

Earnings	Education and Training	Job Outlook

Average	High school	Decreasing

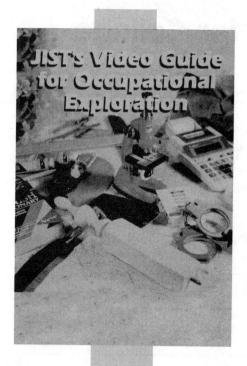

JIST's Video Guide for Occupational Exploration
Real People, Real Jobs, Real Information

The Best Video Series of Its Kind!

Viewers explore careers in 12 major occupational interest areas and see interviews with more than 70 people from all over the United States who work in the profiled jobs. Workers speak frankly about what they like and don't like about their jobs. Includes information on training needed for each occupation.

- **Length:** 15 videos with a run time of approximately 25-30 minutes each
- **Audience:** High School, College, Adult
- **Format:** Informational; serious
- **Category:** Career Exploration
- **Key Characters:** Multicultural

Fifteen-Video Set

ISBN 1-56370-223-1
Order Code JV2231
$729.00

Individual Video Titles: $69.00

Your Career—Introduction to the Series
Artistic Careers
Scientific Careers
Careers with Plants and Animals
Protective Careers
Mechanical Careers, Part One
Mechanical Careers, Part Two
Industrial Careers
Business Detail Careers
Selling Careers
Accommodating Careers
Humanitarian Careers
Leading and Persuading Careers, Part One
Leading and Persuading Careers, Part Two
Physical Performing Careers

The Career Connection for College Education

A Guide to College Education & Related Career Opportunities
By Fred A. Rowe, Ed.D.

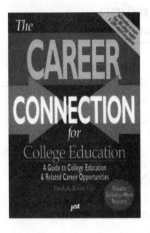

This easy-to-read reference for students and adults provides information on more than 100 college majors and the careers to which they can lead. Each college major description includes information on: types of degrees available, typical courses, prerequisite courses, and average starting salaries.

OTHER INFORMATION
- Includes self-assessment section
- Cross-references each degree to the *Dictionary of Occupational Titles*
- Latest projections of job growth and earnings
- 1,000 occupations cross-referenced to the DOT

ISBN: 1-56370-142-1 • **$16.95** • Order Code: CCCE

The Career Connection for Technical Education

A Guide to Technical Training & Related Career Opportunities
By Fred A. Rowe, Ed.D.

An easy-to-read reference for students and adults that provides information on more than 60 technical majors and the careers to which they can lead. Each degree description includes information on: educational requirements, typical courses, prerequisite courses, average starting salaries.

OTHER INFORMATION
- More than 750 occupations cross-referenced
- Includes self-assessment section
- Cross-references each degree to the *Dictionary of Occupational Titles*
- Covers all major technical careers

ISBN: 1-56370-143-X • **$14.95** • Order Code: CCTE

The Career Exploration Inventory

A Guide for Exploring Work, Leisure, and Learning
By John J. Liptak, Ed.D.

This self-administered assessment device integrates work, learning, *and leisure*. Students reflect on 120 brief activity statements. A simple self-scoring grid gives an immediate picture of interest levels in 15 categories. A 4-panel guide quickly relates test results to occupations, education and training, and *GOE* codes.

A simple, inexpensive, and valuable resource. Available in packages of 25, 12-page folders. No other components needed!

ISBN: 1-56370-063-8 • **Package of 25: $29.95** • Order Code: C6-CEI

Occupational Clues

A Career Interest Survey
Compiled and edited by J. Michael Farr

With six checklists, this assessment device explores job possibilities from several perspectives, including three not specifically work-related. This makes it both thorough and appropriate for those with little or no work experience.

The 24-page version does not require use of any specific occupational reference. The 32-page version includes information on using the *Complete Guide for Occupational Exploration*.

ISBN: 1-56370-088-3 • **32-page Long Form, Pkg. of 25: $48.95** • Order Code: C6-CLUES
ISBN: 1-56370-108-1 • **24-page Short Form, Pkg. of 25: $36.95** • Order Code: C6-SHORT

The World of Work and You

An Innovative Approach to Exploring Career Alternatives

This complete 32-page career and education planning system for youth is ideal for career exploration programs. In-the-book activities help students understand themselves and the importance of setting career and life goals, and teach them to develop action plans.

An excellent resource for middle and high school students, this booklet emphasizes the importance of values and education in career planning.

ISBN: 0-942784-28-6 • **Package of 25: $48.95** • Order Code: C6-WOW

Occupational Outlook Handbook

1996-1997 Edition
By the U.S. Department of Labor

The best reprint available of the most widely used career reference in the country. Completely updated information on the 250 top jobs in our economy. Recommended for job seekers, students, career changers, and business people.

ISBN: 1-56370-278-9 • **Hardcover: $21.95** • Order Code: J2789
ISBN: 1-56370-277-0 • **Softcover: $15.95** • Order Code: J2770

The Complete Guide for Occupational Exploration

Edited by J. Michael Farr with data from the U.S. Department of Labor

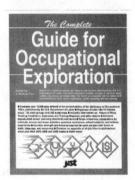

Since its introduction, the *CGOE* has been acclaimed as an essential career reference. Organizes all 12,741 jobs listed in the current *Dictionary of Occupational Titles* into increasingly specific clusters of related jobs. The structure and helpful cross-referencing systems make this an invaluable, easy-to-use resource for anyone exploring career alternatives.

ISBN: 1-56370-100-6 • **Hardcover: $49.95** • Order Code: CGOEH
ISBN: 1-56370-052-2 • **Softcover: $39.95** • Order Code: CGOE

The Enhanced Guide for Occupational Exploration

2nd Edition
By Marilyn Maze and Donald Mayall

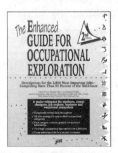

This 1995 revision provides descriptions for 2,800 jobs covering 95% of the workforce. Using the same "interest areas" as the *CGOE*, this book also provides information on worker traits and characteristics needed for each job. A must-have for any career reference library!

ISBN: 1-56370-244-4 • **Hardcover: $44.95** • Order Code: J2444
ISBN: 1-56370-207-X • **Softcover: $34.95** • Order Code: J207X